SOUTHENNAN.
VOL II.

LONDON:
NICHOLS AND SON, 25, PARLIAMENT STREET.

SOUTHENNAN.

BY JOHN GALT, ESQ.

AUTHOR OF

"LAWRIE TODD," "THE ANNALS OF THE PARISH,"

&c. &c.

"When royal Mary, blithe of mood,
Kept holiday in Holyrood."

Hogg.

IN THREE VOLUMES.

VOL. II.

LONDON:

HENRY COLBURN AND RICHARD BENTLEY,
NEW BURLINGTON STREET.

1830.

SOUTHENNAN.

CHAPTER I.

"Dexterity and sufferance
Are engines the pure politic must work with."

FORD.

FOR some time after the Reception, a succession of entertainments were given by the City of Edinburgh to her Majesty and the Court. It was, however, remarked, that she appeared but little disposed to cultivate any intimacy with the families of the nobility. She stood too strictly, it was alleged, on her royalty, and even in her court she formed a small circle of familiars around herself, within which few, even of the most accomplished and esteemed of the

Scottish gentry found admission. The fatality of her ancestors had already overtaken her; and scarcely in any one measure of conduct, or of government, did she appear worthy of the reputation she deservedly enjoyed for intelligence, discernment, and judgment.

Within that little exclusive household circle, Southennan was frequently an honoured guest; but while enjoying the sunshine, he could not behold, without alarm, the clouds arising in the horizon. And yet there appeared no deviation from propriety in the behaviour of Mary, as a gentlewoman: he thought her occasionally, perhaps, too familiar; but from any slight inflexion of conduct of this kind, she resumed her dignity with so much ease and grace, that the aberration only served to extend her influence among those who were favoured with her private countenance.

The bustle and the banquettings, in which the Court was engaged, prevented leisure for particular remarks on the conduct of those by whom the Queen was surrounded; but, nevertheless, the demeanour of Chatelard, though

regulated by extreme caution and delicacy, did not escape the shrewd observation of our hero, to whom it was evident that he lost no opportunity of always appearing in his most attractive colours before her Majesty, while his artificial deference to Adelaide in public was no less manifestly the deliberate effect of systematic study.

It would be to equivocate with the human heart, to say that Southennan beheld the increasing passion of Chatelard without something like gratification; nor did his loyalty much repine, when he perceived that Mary did not rebuke the rash young man with such decision as would have quenched his hopes, but amused herself with his ardour, even while she evinced something like flirtation, if such a term may be applied to the reciprocities of persons so far apart in their respective spheres.

The effect of Southennan's discovery of Chatelard's presumptuous affection, served to nourish his own love for Adelaide. He was persuaded, by many incidents, that she also had perceived the ambition of the accomplished

Frenchman; but he calculated without a sufficient knowledge of the fond feelings by which she was animated, when he fancied, that the hopelessness of her unrequited attachment would extinguish its ardour. This made him patient. Day after day passed with him in jealous vigilance; but the deportment of Mary was so often seemingly equivocal, though only dictated by the suggestions of feminine gaiety and juvenile playfulness, that he could not always repress his persuasion that the Frenchman would ultimately triumph. His confidant was Rizzio.

The ambition of the Italian was piqued by the favour which he thought the Queen evinced for Chatelard: envious in his nature, he dreaded a competitor in the ascendancy which he secretly, with all the zeal of an acute and adventurous spirit, was endeavouring to attain. He was thus his unprovoked enemy, and the fear of being frustrated by his influence chafed his jealousy into hatred. Rizzio in his hate, however, was no less subtile than wary in his ambition. He concealed it as carefully and studied its indulgence with equal solicitude.

Acquainted with the depth to which Southennan was enamoured of Adelaide, he darkly discerned that her passion for the Frenchman might be so managed as to render her Scottish lover subservient to his machinations.

It is mournful to reflect on the cabals which infested the palace of the Scottish Queen; by the ingenuousness of youth, and perhaps also of her nature, she was incapable of suspecting the intrigues, personal and political, by which she was environed. She saw in her counsellors, and the great officers of state, men of harsh feelings, and forbidding countenances, who treated her with less homage than the worship to which she had been accustomed in France; and, save her ladies, she had no advisers in those things which most concerned the graces of her character; for her natural brother, the Prior of St. Andrews, partaking of the austere temper of the time, often in his kindest admonitions, breathed more of restraint than accorded with the vivacity in which she delighted, and which was natural to her age and sex.

Of all her ladies, Adelaide enjoyed her confidence the most; but from the time she had observed her attachment to Chatelard, and suspected his devotion to herself, she assumed a slight though obvious degree of ceremony towards her. This did not escape the searching penetration of Rizzio, but he erred in the construction he put upon it. Knowing the Queen's confidence in Adelaide, and observing that, if not withdrawn, it was suddenly regulated by some occult motive, he ascribed the change to a kindling predilection on the part of Mary for the ill-fated Frenchman.

This apprehension roused his latent energies. The slightest manifestation of affection, on the part of the Queen, he foresaw would be ruin to his anticipations, for he knew that Chatelard stood in some awe of him, and with that sinister wisdom which often overreaches itself, he apprehended, that were Chatelard once possessed of influence enough over the Queen, to move her to any measure, he would not long be allowed to remain in her service. A simple incident soon brought these anxieties into action.

One day as her Majesty was descending the stairs, attended, accidentally, by himself and Chatelard on her right and left, followed by Adelaide and the Lady Mary Livingstone, she slightly stumbled. The Italian instantly offered his arm, but she took hold of the Frenchman's. It was an act of the moment, unpremeditated, and done without intentional favour or distinction, but it seemed not so to the seething spirit of Rizzio. He beheld in it an indication which his adversary would construe into a mark of special favour, as he believed it was intended to be; and from that moment the unhappy fortunes of the Frenchmen were determined.

Rizzio brooded over the incident, as if it had discovered to him something which he had not before suspected. With the ingenious cunning of his nature, like the wounded scorpion, he struck the venom into himself, and writhed with agonies of his own infliction. Though his apprehensions were, perhaps, not altogether imaginary, they were yet beyond reason, for Chatelard was not envious, and his passion for the Queen was too much of a blaze, shooting up

from vanity, to have respect to aught save its own object. He might occasionally be uneasy at observing the vigilance with which the Italian's dark and piercing eye followed him; but there was a quality in his passion, arising from the direction it had taken, that gave generosity to all his thoughts. The insane fancy of gaining the Queen's affections, filled him with vast ideas of liberality and munificence.

CHAPTER II.

"Deliver with more openness your answers
To my demands."
SHAKSPEARE.

On the evening after the little incident mentioned in the last chapter, Rizzio took occasion to throw himself in the way of Southennan, without appearing to have sought him, although the meeting was the result of study and contrivance. In the management of such seeming accidents the sinister Italian was ingeniously expert.

It happened to be Friday, a day which the Queen always passed in a more sequestered manner than any other of the week, save on the high festivals of her religion. Her household circle was not assembled in the evening: only her ladies were admitted to her; for even her

ministers were directed not to disturb her retirement, unless their business was urgent, and could not be postponed without detriment to the State. Her attendants, those of the chosen number, were in consequence at liberty to amuse themselves as they thought fit. Southennan on these nights rarely went to the palace, for Adelaide was generally on them the preferred companion of her royal mistress. Rizzio had noticed this, and planned his machination accordingly.

It had been his custom to dine occasionally at the Unicorn with the foreigners by whom the table was frequented, and where he knew our hero was almost a regular daily guest. He went there at the usual hour, and, as if he had no particular wish for conversation with Southennan, he took his place at dinner on the opposite side of the table, and discussed with those around him, in the apparent ease of a disengaged mind, the various topics which chance or remark suggested. Even after dinner, and when several of the guests had departed, he evinced no disposition to move nearer to Southennan;

but he sometimes particularly addressed him across the table, as it were in reply to some opinion in which he affected to differ from him.

In this apparently unpremeditated manner he continued to act, until he perceived a disposition on the part of Southennan to rise, when he dextrously turned the conversation on some one of the many topics of the day by which the minds of all men were then agitated, expressing himself with a degree of confidence on the subject which drew from our hero an equally decided reply. A controversy was the consequence, which Rizzio managed with so much zeal, that although there was not the slightest approximation to a quarrel between them, their conversation was yet so little agreeable to the other gentlemen in the room, that they one by one dropped away, and left the apartment to the disputants.

When Rizzio had thus obtained for themselves exclusive possession of the room, he suddenly paused, and looking suspiciously to the right and left, moved from the place where he sat at dinner, and took a seat beside our hero.

The abruptness of the pause, the jealous vigilance with which he cast his eyes around, and something singular and emphatic in his manner, were greatly calculated to rouse attention.

"I hope," said the Italian, with a whispering earnestness, "that nothing during dinner nor since, in my manner towards you, has indicated any particular desire for such an opportunity as this, to speak with you in confidence."

Southennan was surprised at the observation, and naturally enough remarked in reply, that he could not imagine a cause or an occasion for so much address to procure an opportunity for a confidential conversation with him; for the candour of his mind did not allow him to suspect, or rather to understand that the art of Rizzio's explanation might be the effect of design, and calculated to augment the impression of what he had to communicate.

"I am glad it is so," said Rizzio; "and I trust that those who last left us are persuaded we were on the eve of a quarrel, or at least were not likely to have had either treason or conspiracy to arrange."

" Treason!" exclaimed Southennan, " to what do you allude?" and he said this firmly, for he thought the conduct of his companion more curiously ingenious than any thing between them could possibly require.

" Hush! speak lower," murmured Rizzio, raising his hand, and assuming a knotted and significant look; " What we have both feared, and perhaps one of us wished for, is not far off."

" Explain yourself, Rizzio; I am incapable of comprehending the meaning of this mystery."

" Did you not first point out to my attention the sensual ardour of Chatelard's devotion to the Queen?"

" What of that?" inquired Southennan eagerly, with an accent of anxiety, almost of alarm, dreading he might have said too much upon the subject, or been treacherously dealt with; for it was not to the Italian alone that he had spoken of the Frenchman's presumptuous attachment, but to others he had been also jocular; to Rizzio only had he expressed any feeling of interest or apprehension on the subject.

"Let us not talk of it, nor mention names more than may be necessary," rejoined Rizzio; "I have myself noted it, until a conviction has been wrought as perfect as your own. But ――――" and, in pausing, he again looked eagerly and apprehensively around.

"Well! what would you say?"

"I believe you, Southennan, to be an honourable man, and my friend; but there are things which ought only to be spoken of by the eyes. My fortune, my life perhaps, hang upon what I have to tell; cannot you hear my thoughts?"

"Perhaps I do," replied Southennan, a little drily, displeased at being distrusted; "but speak out. I do not despair that fidelity shall win its reward."

"You have said it," exclaimed Rizzio, with a hollow and suppressed shout, as it were, of triumph.

"You say not so?" said Southennan.

"It were perdition to us both to breathe the mildew and the blight that might be in the infectious answer to your question," said the

Italian solemnly; adding, less seriously, "I did not say the love had yet met return,—had yet——."

"It would be cause enough," replied our hero fervently, "to make the chaste spirit of Adelaide quit——"

"Hush! Let not your tongue give utterance to what you have imagined; steal the best pearl from the crown rather than breathe such an imputation. I beseech you, Southennan, to ask no better knowledge than you have guessed; but let us consider how it may advantage your own cause.—Nothing, I fear!"

"Unless it can be made known to Adelaide," rejoined Southennan thoughtfully, adding, "how may that be? She will herself find it out!"

"I fear, Southennan, we both stand in jeopardy: knowing and not to tell. Are not you friendly with the Prior of St. Andrews?"

"Would you have me speak to him?" cried Southennan, starting, "after having so warned me how near akin the thing is to treason. He will call for proof; what have we, but conjecture: and with conjecture only, dare we

impeach the honour of the Queen? This matter is not yet ripe even for talk, Rizzio."

" I said not that it was so," replied the Italian; " but only thought it might soon be."

Here their conversation was interrupted by the return of some of the gentlemen who had dined with them.

CHAPTER III.

> "Thus I take off the shroud in which my cares
> Are folded up from view of common eyes."
>
> THE BROKEN HEART.

SOUTHENNAN and Rizzio left the Unicorn together. The Italian went to the palace, and our hero to his own lodgings.

It was by this time late in the afternoon; the sun had indeed set, and the twilight was advancing. The streets were in consequence thronged as usual in Edinburgh at that time of the day, with handicraftsmen and apprentices.

In passing up the High-street, Southennan, not being much accustomed to thread the mazes of a crowd, felt himself a good deal pushed about, especially near the Cross, where the assemblage was numerous and restless. At the entrance of a narrow closs, where the people were thickest,

an old man addressed him by name, and begged he would follow him.

Something in the appearance and voice of the stranger excited at once his attention and curiosity, and he followed him down the close, and up a Jacob's-ladder ascent of stairs, to the eleventh story of one of the Babel edifices that overlooked the North Loch.

The appearance of the old man, as he walked before him, seemed to Southennan to be something remarkable. He had evidently been of a stout frame, and his limbs were well formed and firm, but his steps were tottering and unequal, and the bend in his shoulder shewed more of a stoop than decrepitude. When they reached the top of the highest stair the stranger opened the door with a key, and through a dark passage conducted him to a small room cheerfully lighted by a window which was open, and which commanded a view of the magnificent landscape that spreads from the city towards the northwest.

When they were in this room, and the door shut, the old man requested Southennan to be

seated, and, with a smile, pulled down his beard, and shewed the face and features of Knockwhinnie.

Our hero laughed at the revelation, and said—

" I could not have thought it possible that one so robust could have assumed so much of the infirm appearance of eild."

" Ah !" replied the Outlaw, " Time will allow us to anticipate his triumphs, but he has put it out of our power ever to imitate youth. I have, however, only time to tell you briefly of my voyage. It was but this morning that the vessel in which I returned reached Leith roads, and since then I have been eagerly in quest of you without success. I was returning to these lodgings when I happened to observe you in the crowd ; it is fortunate that we have met so soon. Have you been able to supersede my outlawry?"

Southennan did not return a direct answer. He only expressed his satisfaction at seeing Knockwhinnie again so well, and trusted that his enquiries were calculated to appease the

disordered feelings with which he had been so long afflicted.

" Then you have not," said the Outlaw, " procured either remission or pardon. What have you done in the business?"

Southennan looked confused. He had literally effected nothing; not altogether from neglect, but from a feeling of procrastination, induced by his unsatisfactory mediation with Dufroy, and from a wish to avoid any explanation concerning the reluctance of Dufroy to lend his assistance.

" So!" cried Knockwhinnie; " you have not been able to do anything for me. Well, it can't be helped! But have you learned any thing likely to mitigate the pain of this disappointment?"

" Tell me first," replied Southennan, " what has been the result of your own visit to Normandy; for you went off at an unlucky hour."

Knockwhinnie looked a little grave at this question, which seemed to him something like an evasion; but giving his head a slight toss, as if

to shake off something disagreeable, he replied, " Perhaps you say justly; for I met with nothing of which I might not have better ascertained the facts here. My wife is dead—some years ago she died; and my child has been brought up in the family of Count Dufroy. Instead of doing me wrong, he has, in his kindness to Adelaide, been my greatest benefactor. By his influence with the late King Francis, the husband of our Mary, he procured my Adelaide to be placed among the honourable attendants of the Queen; and the occasion of his visit is to restore her to the family of her mother. Have you seen her?"

Southennan replied, with emphasis, that he had, and that she had inspired him with the most ardent affection, which he hoped would be approved by her father.

"What says she herself?" exclaimed Knockwhinnie, eagerly, at the same time holding out his hand in token of his satisfaction at the news.

But Southennan again looked exceedingly confused, and was about to make some general reply.

"Deal plainly with me!" cried the Outlaw. "Is there any obstacle on her part to your union?"

The straightforwardness of Knockwhinnie admitted of no equivocation; and, in consequence, our hero found himself constrained to speak of what he had observed in the conduct of Adelaide.

Knockwhinnie listened to him evidently with greedy ears: his eyes were seemingly cast on the ground; but they were abstracted, and took no heed of aught within the scope of their vision. He leant forward, resting his hands upon his knees, and presented altogether an appearance of intense and anxious attention.

When the recital was finished, he continued for some time in the same posture, and silent. At last he said, half, as it were, in soliloquy, without lifting his eyes, "Dufroy requires atonement from me, before I can hope for his assistance to procure the reversal of my outlawry!"

Southennan, who had been speaking with warmth and tenderness of Adelaide, was surprised at the irrelevancy of her father's remark,

and found himself, as it were, constrained to say, " I was speaking of your daughter."

" True—true—I heard you," replied Knockwhinnie; "but something must be done before we talk of that. This Chatelard, of whom you have been telling me, must be got rid of." And, in saying these words, he unconsciously darted a keen look at Southennan, the effect of which on him was such a hurried recollection of the conversation he had so shortly before held with Rizzio, that it touched him with something like alarm; and he exclaimed, with a voice of dread, " How rid of him?"

The Outlaw looked at him sternly. " I think, Southennan, that by this time you should have known that I do not regard the dagger as always the best means."

Southennan saw that he had touched harshly upon a tender string. But the construction which Knockwhinnie had put upon his words could not be easily obviated, without mentioning the attachment of Chatelard to the Queen.

The Outlaw, seeing his embarrassment, subjoined, " I do not, however, wonder at your

question. Only there has not been enough of provocation, even in the feigned affection for my daughter, committed by this Chatelard, to justify an appeal to violent courses. But, as I have said, we cannot yet talk of that, as my esteem for you would prompt me. I therefore have only to beseech you, before any suspicion is entertained of my return, to bring Count Dufroy and myself together. I am his debtor, and must humble myself to obtain an acquittance of the debt. I have done him an injury; it is necessary that I should atone for it. I pray you, for the affection you profess for Adelaide, that you lose no time in this business: let it be done, if possible, to-night. Do go at once, and I shall wait here an answer, or your return."

CHAPTER IV.

"I saw a smith stand with his hammer, thus,
The whilst his iron did on the anvil cool,
With open mouth, swallowing a tailor's news."
SHAKSPEARE.

IN proceeding from Knockwhinnie's lodgings Southennan met his boy.

"Ah! Laird," exclaimed Hughoc, on seeing him: "do ye ken what a come-to-pass has happened? Knockwhinnie's back frae France; and sic a like sight! ye wouldna' ken him were ye to see him in your spoon."

Our hero was a little startled, apprehensive lest the Outlaw might have been discovered by some other person.

"How came you," said he, "to know this? Who told you?"

"Na," replied the boy; "I'se warrant naebody

told me; but ye see, I chanced to hae a needcessity about the horses, so I was down at Widow Hutchie's house, and standing at the door, glowering frae me, there came an auld gaberlunzie looking man wi' a white beard, that would hae been creditable to the auldest he-goat in Arran, and leaning on his staff, which was a very pretty ane, and, I daur say, had a sword in its kyte, for it had a silver virl just below the heft lith, he asked me, wi' a kind o' strangulated voice, if I could tell him where young Southennan was to be found. 'I ken but ae Southennan,' quo' I; and I looked up in his face, and as his mouth was open, I discerned by his teeth that he was na' sae auld as he was like, and hadna' lost mark o' mouth; so a jealousy fell upon me, and I thought, wha can this guisart be?"

"Speak to the point," interrupted his master.

"Well," resumed Hughoc, "speaking to the point: I looked a little better at him; but really his face was sae weel hidden aneath a coat o' paint, that for the leeving soul o' me, I couldna' guess wha it possibly could be; but it cam into my head to cry wi' a loud skreigh o' terror,

' Eh! gudeman, there's a jenny-wi'-the-many-feet crawling on your coat-neck. 'The deevil there is!' said he, in his natural voice: and wha's natural voice, think ye, was that, Laird? As sure 's death, it was Knockwhinnie's! Seeing he wasna' disposed to be confidential wi' me, I didna let on that I kent him, but just said, that ye were down at the Abbey gallanting wi' the Queen and her leddies."

"Well," replied his master, "you have shewn yourself, Hughoc, both shrewd and sharp; but tell nobody what you have discovered."

"Ye needna' counsel that," exclaimed the boy. "Wha would I tell? Ye surely, Laird, dinna think me so lost to discretion as to speak on sic a kittle point wi' our Baldy, wha, for any thing that I see, is growing to be a monk. Hech! but it's a puir trade now-a-days. He'll no make his plack a bawbee by that."

This information respecting his servant a little molested the tranquillity of Southennan, although it was not altogether new to him. He had remarked something like remissness in the

conduct of Baldy from the first day of their arrival in Edinburgh, and he thought him too particular in his attendance on Father Jerome, who he well knew was stirring among the Catholic priesthood; the arrival of the Queen having drawn them in great numbers to the town. Being, however, anxious to complete his mission to Count Dufroy, he ordered Hughoc to attend him to the palace, and, as they went down the Canongate, he inquired his reason for supposing that Baldy was likely to turn a monk.

"Oh! oh!" said the boy: "I didna' mean that he was sic a desperate sneck-drawer as to turn a true monk; I only meant that he was growing ane in a certain sense. But, Laird, I would look weel about me if I were you; for I heard Father Jerome tell a muckle fat painchy priest that he had but sma' expectation o' you, and the utmost it would be in his power to do was, wi' the help o' Baldy, to keep you frae falling into harm's way, which they meant was going to the orthodox kirks!"

Southennan bit his lips at hearing this; the idea of being so circumvented by his servant

provoked his indignation, but he only said to the boy in an indifferent tone—

"And how did you overhear this conversation?"

"Ye see, Sir, I hae sometimes naething to do, and so whiles I dauner about, and whiles I gang in till Widow Hutchie's room, and lie down on the big kist that stands ahint the door, and make a bit skip frae care into the land o' Nod. Nae farther gane than yesterday, being in the humour for a doze of forgetfulness, I lay down on the kist lid, and when I was lying there, in came Father Jerome wi' that haggis-bellied monk, and they were unco couthy and cosy, talking into ane anither's lugs about papistical matters. Now I like, when I see folk sae earnest, to get some notion o' what the're saying, and Baldy just gae's wud whenever he catches me wi' my lug at the keyhole. 'Od, Laird! but the body has turned unco cankery; howsomever, that's nane o' our business even now. But when I saw the twa enter the room, I snored wi' a' my might, and closed my eyne. 'Puir chicken,' said the round-about friar, 'he's tired,

let him alone;" for Father Jerome was going to waken me. Then they sat down and they had—Lord Laird! but fat priests are aye dry—they had a chappin o' the Luckie's best, and they spoke, and they better spoke, and ye would hae thought that they had a' the cares o' Scotland on their backs, and the sins o' the warld likewise; sae frae less to mair, they couldna' weel do without haeing a rug at your tail. That's just the way that I overheard them."

The peculiarities of Hughoc and his natural shrewdness had often amused his master, who began to think that he had been progressing since they had come to Edinburgh; and this, as they walked along, induced him to enquire what the boy thought of the town and people.

" The town," said Hughoc, " is weel enough, for I fancy a' towns are naturally dirty; but as for the folk, I dinna think the're right folk at a'. In the country, if ye're weary, or dry, or hungry, ye may gang in to a neighbour's house, and rest yoursel', or seek a drink o' milk or a bite o' bread. 'Od, Sir! this is a faminous place; and then the're a' sae wise; Gude keep us, but the folk

o' Embro' are wise folk, considering their ignorance!"

"However, Hughoc, no doubt you find them very civil?"

"Ceevil! 'od Laird, they ken nae mair o' ceevility than stupit stots. There was twa' o' them; ane a man wi' a bailie's belly, and anither wi' his hosen up o'er his breek knees, wi' a green apron and a red nightcap, threads about his neck, swatches in the ae hand, and a pair o' muckle shears in the ither, holding a discourse concerning the Queen's Majesty; and the tailoring man, that was him wi' the shears, said to the other that he was mista'en if he supposed a papistical princess like the Queen, could be any better than a malefactoring nun amang friars. Hearing this, I stopped and turned up my lug to kep what they were saying. Weel, it's dreadfu' how they daur't to touch me! but the lean man wi' the nightcap and the shears, gied me sic a pelt on the head that he dunkeled my hernpan, and the man that was sae big wi' belly lifted up his foot, and—"

"What did he do?" inquired our hero; for

Hughoc paused, as if suddenly afraid to tell more, but encouraged by the question, he cried,

"Do! I just took haud o' him by the leg, and he was down on the breadth o' his back on the causey stanes without controversy."

"You will get yourself into trouble, if you dare to do such things," said his master, laughing.

"'Deed, Laird, that's as true as the reformed gospel."

"How?" exclaimed Southennan; "what do you know of the reformed or unreformed gospel?"

"Weel, Laird, if ye'll no be angry, I'll tell you the truth; it was ordained that I should go by Giles's kirk last Sabbath."

"Ordained, and Sabbath!" ejaculated Southennan.

"Just sae, Laird, and nae harm in't. Sae going past the kirk door, I heard a bum-bizzing within; and could do nae less than look in; and there I beheld a divine, hallooing at a dreadfu' rate against what he called—'Od! I doubt he'll get his fairing for't hereafter—the idolatry o' the mass. But ae thing he made plain to me, that it couldna' be an idolatry; for by the eyne he

convinced everybody bread and wine wasna' flesh and bluid;—now, Laird, I'm o' that way o' thinking. And he told us that unless we made use o' our senses, the scales could never be removed from off the eyes o' the understanding. But when I got hame, and told Baldy what I had heard, he loupit like a blackbird, and gied me sic a skelp o' persecution on the haffit, that I think it did weel to reform me."

By this time they had crossed the gutter that marked the boundary of the sanctuary of the palace, within which a considerable crowd was assembled round a tall, strapping, randy-looking woman.

"Eh! pater-noster!" exclaimed Hughoc, "it's Friar Michael."

CHAPTER V.

" Thus I talk wisely, and to purpose."
            THE LOVER'S MELANCHOLY.

Southennan, enjoining Hughoc to remain for him at the portal, went into the Palace; but it would have been a strong injunction indeed, which, on such an occasion, would have curtailed the freedom of that boy's will. The transformation of Auchenbrae had deeply interested his curiosity; and he mingled with the crowd, around the apparent termagant.

The appearance of Auchenbrae at that time and in that disguise, so near the Palace, was not altogether voluntary. He had been out on some of his wild rambles, beyond the water of Leith, and in returning across the ferry, had been recognised by Johnnie Gaff and one of his compeers, who happened to be present, and who

attempted to seize him. But he rescued himself, and, gathering up the petticoats of his disguise, ran from them across the Links to the Sanctuary of Holyrood Chapel.

Being the first who had taken refuge there since the purification of the church, the crowd were in doubt whether he could be taken without the bounds, and carried before the magistrates, and one among them maintained the legal impracticability of violating the Sanctuary; but Johnnie Gaff, who was the Orator of the human race on the occasion, with his lips quivering, his face pale with passion, and his eyes as if they would have kindled candles, holding the delinquent by the throat, denied the doctrine as a papistical abomination.

" I will prove it," exclaimed Johnnie; " and I call in the Queen's name for the *Posse Com-a-to-us* to implement the caption. This is a case o' reestment *jurisdictiony fundandy*, and no question *quoad privilegy* can be raised on it."

In the midst, however, of Johnnie's oration, the disturbance had roused the Palace-guard; which, without respect of persons, laid hold of

Auchenbrae as well as the orators, and dragged them to the guard-house. In vain did Johnnie plead his privilege as a halberdier of the Lord Provost: the soldiers only laughed at him. Auchenbrae, who in the mean time, had all his eyes about him, was eagerly looking for an opportunity to escape; and having been much incommoded by his female garments, he was quietly untying his petticoats, the easier to shoot out from among them.

Johnnie Gaff, in the mean time, was waxing more and more wroth at the irreverence of the soldiers, and threatening them with all sorts of pains and penalties, for the indignity with which, in his person, they treated the authority and jurisdiction of the Provost, Bailies, and Council of the Burgh of Edinburgh. His menaces, however, only served to increase their derision; in the midst of which, the door being accidentally left open, the culprit dropt his petticoats, and was off like an arrow from the bow.

" Gude guide us," exclaimed Johnnie, cooled in an instant, " he's *fugæ* again, wi' neither kilt nor breeks !"

This new escape had the effect of instantly clearing the guard-house: but none of the soldiers followed. Johnnie Gaff, however, as if he had been booted in seven-league boots, rushed after the fugitive like the nucleus of a comet, with a spreading train of children, huzzaing and cheering him forward.

The condition of Auchenbrae deterred him from running far into the town. He ascended the first outside stair, and darted into a room where an elderly female was spinning on a distaff, and singing, at the open window. Without leave asked, he bounded into a bed which stood in a corner, and drew the coverlet over him.

Scarcely was he in this asylum, when the noise of his pursuers rose loud in the street, by which the industrious housewife was moved to look out, and, on seeing them, to call aloud—

"Hey gudeman!" and, licking her fingers, she twirled her whorl, and cried still louder, "Hey, Johnnie Gaff, there's a wud woman in our bed! Come and tak' her out immedintly."

But Johnnie flew still onward, regardless of the cool cry of his wife. Auchenbrae heard

what she said, and called to her for goodness' sake to make no noise, but to come in and lend him a petticoat, for which he would reward her. On hearing his hoarse masculine voice, she was so startled, that she flung her distaff from her, and ran down the stair, crying "Robbery and murder!" At the same moment, Auchenbrae chanced to observe Johnnie's best breeches, and all the paraphernalia of the full dress in which he attended the magistrates to church on Sundays, hanging behind the door. His case admitted of no delay: he sprung from the bed, tore off the remainder of his female vestments, and was soon clothed in the garb of the Provost's chief halberdier.

By this time Lucky Gaff had roused the neighbourhood; the men and children had followed the chase, but the wives joined her: and, just as she was leading this army of auxiliaries to the stair-foot, Auchenbrae made his appearance on the top, dressed as her husband.

"Eh! it's my gudeman's wraith," cried she, and fell back with the terror of astonishment

into the arms of one of her kimmers; while Auchenbrae, dashing boldly through them, was again free.

Meanwhile, Hughoc, in total oblivion of his master's orders, was one of the most forward and eager of the hounds in the hunt; but his sagacity had soon apprised him that they had lost the scent, and that the fox was earthed. Anxious to tell Johnnie this, he kept crying aloud behind him, " Stop, stop, stop him!" At this juncture, Knockwhinnie, unable to repress his anxiety to meet our hero, was coming down the street in his disguise, crippling slowly, in the twilight. The sound struck his ear; and, being instantly alarmed, he forgot his assumed infirmities, and ran with the speed and agility so necessary to an Outlaw. The chase was turned. Johnnie, on seeing the new game, rushed upon Knockwhinnie, and, seizing him by the collar, held him fast. Among the foremost of the crowd by whom they were instantly surrounded, was Hughoc, who exclaimed, on seeing who was taken,

" Eh, what a pity!" and darted away, while

the Outlaw was conducted to the Council Chamber.

In the meantime, Southennan had ascended the palace-stairs, and was waiting in the gallery for the Count Dufroy, who was then engaged with the Queen; and, as he was standing there, Adelaide came from her own apartment.

"I have great news for you," said he, addressing her. "This morning, your father returned from France. We must, without delay, endeavour to procure his pardon. Though the Count refuses to assist, I trust he will do nothing to mar our application."

The news, and the abruptness of the communication, so affected her, that she was for some time unable to speak, until relieved by a burst of tears.

"Where is he?" was her first exclamation. "Let me but see him—take me to him!"

Southennan replied, it could not be that night; "for," said he, "although it might facilitate what we so earnestly desire, were he taken, yet a reasonable doubt hangs upon it. If taken, he will be brought to trial, and the Queen,

so soon after her arrival, will hesitate to interfere until his trial shall have been completed. And should he be found"——

"Oh!" cried Adelaide; "say not the dreadful possibility. I will this night myself supplicate the Queen."

More she would have said; but Chatelard and Rizzio came into the gallery. And at their appearance Southennan softly cried, "Hush!" and made a signal for her to be silent.

CHAPTER VI.

"Now came still evening on, and twilight grey
Had in her sober livery all things clad."

MILTON.

THE twilight was almost faded when Auchenbrae escaped in the habiliments of Johnnie Gaff. As he could hardly expect to pass up into the town unremarked, he directed his flight across the King's Park, and ascended the road which led to the chapel of St. Anthony, to wait on the mountain until the darkness of the night would allow him to return in safety to his lodgings.

The original character of this profligate man was not without qualities which might have been improved into virtues. He possessed, besides an impassioned admiration of female beauty,

extreme sensibility to the charms of external nature. In the midst of his wildness there was much of poesy, and in consequence the contrition which he sometimes felt for his licentiousness was often blended with an elegance of sentiment, strangely, as it seemed by its sadness, at variance with the tenor of his life. His excursion across the water of Leith had been one of those loose and low enterprises in which he sometimes recklessly indulged; but the humiliation to which he had been exposed at the Palace Gate, so derogatory to his birth, deeply moved him when alone on the solitude of Arthur's seat.

He continued to ascend the hill until he reached the summit, and sat down looking towards the west, where a faint amber tinge still glowed along the horizon. It was just enough to shew the contour of the Highland mountains, and the brighter and darker masses of the rising grounds and the hollows between. All the dome of the heavens was unclouded, pure azure, in which the stars were numerously kindling. But where the twilight lingered, horizontal streaks of black vapour, recalled gloomy associations of the free day, as seen from

within through the bars and gratings of a prison window.

The sullied fancies of Auchenbrae yielded to the influences of the scene. The memory of youthful times and sunny days and purer thoughts returned, and with a feeling of disgust at himself, he courted, as it were in revenge of his own folly, sullen resolutions, not of amendment, but to hasten the conclusion of his dishonorable career.

As he sat in this desolate mood, leaning forward with his chin resting upon his hand, his abstraction was broken by the sudden apparition of a splendid meteor, trailing its golden fires in a beautiful arch across the heavens. His eyes eagerly followed its course, until it was suddenly shattered into momentary stars, and extinguished. He viewed it as an emblem of his life, a brilliant promise, ending without fulfiling one hope of the admiration that had attended his outset.

In these gloomy ruminations the recollection of the injury he had done to Knockwhinnie was one of the keenest and the deepest. It was the molten fire of the remorse of the moment, and

its lurid gleam changed the hue of his reflections. The anguish of its intensity became as it were an impulse, rather than a motive, to redeem the past; and he rose with the intention of proceeding at once to the magistrates, to acknowledge the extent of his aggression, and afterwards to return to Kilwinning, where he had, from the time of the outrage, assumed the the garb of the Cistertian order, and where, although the great edifice of the monastery had been destroyed by the Reformers, many of the brotherhood continued to reside in the village. But this determination was, like all the promptings of his feeling, an evanescent flash. Throughout the kingdom there was no longer a religious house remaining in which piety or penitence could find refuge. His mind was thus turned to consider the state and circumstances of the times, and he resumed his seat to reflect in what way by them he might retrieve in some degree his long abandoned ambition for fame. But even this flickering of virtue was soon over; the tainted habitude of his thoughts gradually returned, and the spirit of the solitary mountain

and the solemn hour departed. The moral inspiration of the scene passed away; and with the cold contemplation of an artist's eye, he looked only at the forms and outlines of the material things before him; among which, the dark masses and huge lineaments of the city, sprinkled all over with lights, interested his imagination the most. He traced fantastical resemblances in them to the unreal creations of necromancy; but still, as often as he embodied these dreamy images, something haunted him of a melancholy cast. The emotion he had felt was, it is true, at rest, but it was like the calm of the sea, which reflects all objects above and around it. Above and around him were the solemnities of the heavens and the earth, the ocean and the murmurings of a great city, all in the shadows and mysteries of night.

By this time the glow in the west was entirely faded, and he was admonished by a faint brightening in the eastern horizon that he ought to seek his lodging before the moon rose, and while there was yet darkness in the streets to conceal his disguise. He accordingly returned

down from the brow of the hill, and hastened by all the crooked wynds in which he was least exposed to observation, to the house of his kinswoman, which he reached unmolested. But just as he was on the point of entering to ascend the stair, he was met by Johnnie Gaff and Hughoc, and Southennan himself, all proceeding to the Council Chamber.

The boy was the first who observed him, and exclaimed,

" Oh Laird, here's anither officer ! "

With an instinctive grasp, Johnnie Gaff instantly seized the fugitive with both his hands. Auchenbrae, being a more powerful man, might easily have disentangled himself from the tall and meagre halberdier, but his good genius was at that time hovering at hand, and he submitted to be taken prisoner without an effort.

" Who is it ?" exclaimed Southennan.

" Oh, Christal ! it's Friar Michael," replied Hughoc.

" Its the deevil incarnate in *pro. per.* and my best breeks and coat," exclaimed Johnnie Gaff;

for his wife had in the meantime informed him of the robbery; "but Clootie hae his will o' me if he slips through my fingers afore I hae him forenent the Provost, Bailies, and Council of the Burgh o' Embro, to answer *in foro*, for haimsucken in the house o' Kinlochie and stouthrief in mine. My word, but ye're braw in you barrow't feathers! but ye shall mak a *cessy bonorum*, before the night be an hour aulder."

Auchenbrae was not acquainted with Southennan, but discerning by the lights of one of the bowets which had been recently put up in the streets for lamps, his gentlemanly bearing and garb, said,

"Sir, by your appearance I am emboldened to claim your protection. I beg you will, therefore, request this rude fellow to remove his hands: I give you my honour to follow him quietly; but I will not submit to be treated as a common sorner. I am a gentleman."

Against this appeal Johnnie clamorously remonstrated, venting a tirade of maledictions and accusations, interlarded with Latin, so ex-

travagant, that even Auchenbrae himself could not preserve the gravity suitable to his situation. Southennan laughed heartily, and told Johnnie that he would be answerable for the quiet attendance of his prisoner.

"Weel, Sir," replied Johnnie, a little softened by the manner of Southennan, "since ye'll no be an *amicus coorie*, and help me, ye maun gie me caution *judicy sisty*, afore I can part wi' him; and a consideration as a *solatium*, for the damage and detriment done to my breeks."

Southennan drew his purse, and presented Johnnie with a piece of money; at the sight of which Hughoc exclaimed,

"Oh man, but ye hae your ain luck!"

"Hush!" said his master, "take no notice of what I do."

"Steek your eyne, ye deevil's buckie," said Johnnie, soothed by the liberality of Southennan, adding jocularly, "it's an unco thing that a man canna earn an honest penny in this world, without stirring up an *animus injurandy*."

Matters being thus accommodated the party proceeded to the Council Chamber, and as Auchenbrae walked with Johnnie, the children remarked as they passed along, " Eh ! hasna' the town gotten a new Johnnie Gaff? "

CHAPTER VII.

"Courts can give nothing to the wise and good
But scorn of pomp and love of solitude."
YOUNG.

It is now necessary to explain what had come to pass in the meantime, after Hughoc had seen the arrest of Knockwhinnie. His own neglect of his master's injunctions was recollected with alarm, and he ran back to the Palace, in case he should have been missed. He was there, however, long before his master made his appearance at the portal.

Southennan had been detained by Count Dufroy, who almost immediately after Chatelard and Rizzio had joined Adelaide and him in the gallery, came from his audience with the Queen. The Count, on approaching them, discovered something embarrassed in the appearance of Adelaide and our hero, and rightly

conjectured that the other two had come upon them unexpectedly. Being a clear-sighted man of the world, he perceived that it would not be fit, before the intruders, as he deemed them, to inquire the cause of the perplexity, which was, indeed, as obvious to them as to himself. He accordingly said to Adelaide, that the Queen was alone, and he would conduct her to her Majesty, giving, at the same time, a significant look to Southennan, to intimate that he would return to him. He then took Adelaide by the hand to lead her away, and was followed to the door by Chatelard, who evidently intended to go in with them; but the Count stopped before opening it, and, turning round, said, with a countenance of cool dignity,

"The Queen has given directions respecting the hours when she will receive her private company. I have not had time to make her commands known to the household; but you will have the goodness, in the mean time, to obey them."

Chatelard returned in considerable confusion towards our hero and Rizzio, but did not remain

long with them. On some pretence of business to be done before supper, he retired to his own apartment.

During this short scene, Rizzio, in a look which he gave to our hero, disclosed a degree of exultation of which the cause was not apparent; but, as soon as Chatelard quitted the gallery, the Italian took hold of Southennan by the arm, and led him into the bay of one of the remotest windows.

"This," said he, alluding to the communication which the Count Dufroy had made to Chatelard, "was becoming necessary."

"Why? how, necessary?"

Rizzio then told him, that he had deemed it his duty to acquaint Dufroy of what he had observed in the freedom with which Chatelard often regarded the Queen; and that that just and correct nobleman had expressed to him a determination to speak to her Majesty on the subject.

"He has done so, I doubt not," said Southennan; "and the order he has received is the fruit."

"I think so too," replied Rizzio; "and it shows that her Majesty may be advised, even in her passions."

"It does more, in my opinion," said Southennan; "it shows that she does not entertain that attachment which you suspected."

"Do you think so?" inquired Rizzio, with one of his dark, sinister, keen, piercing looks.

"What else should I think?"

Rizzio at once assumed his more usual mask of gaiety, and replied, with a disengaged smile,

"I should have thought, Southennan, that you had known more of woman. May not this very order of the Queen have been given only to lull the suspicions of the Count, and to prevent her partiality from being discovered. It is not so difficult to arrange an intercourse that may not be observed, and at the same time to keep this assurance of decorum to the eye."

"You judge too suspiciously of the sex," was Southennan's answer, expressed in a tone of reserve; for there was something in the address which Rizzio had displayed in the affair, so very like design, that he did not much like it. It had

been his resolution to keep aloof from all court intrigue, and he was a little troubled to find himself so near the hazard of being involved in one of the deepest, perhaps most dangerous.

"But, Southennan, let me ask you one question," said Rizzio. "You have told me of your attachment to Adelaide, and its hopelessness while hers, so manifest for Chatelard, continues; and yet, when we came in upon you just now, there were tears and confidence, and other very lover-like symptoms between you: what was the cause?"

Southennan had preserved, with all but the Count and Adelaide, a studied silence with respect to Knockwhinnie, although, once or twice, he had almost resolved to take the advice of Rizzio, for whose remarkable discernment and dexterity of management he had a high opinion. This question decided him; and he laid the whole case before the Italian.

Rizzio listened with great attention. He made no observation while Southennan was speaking; but when our hero expressed his wonder at the reluctance evinced by Count

Dufroy to interfere with the outlawry, he once or twice looked eagerly, as if something was passing in his mind; and a smile, not expressive of any satisfaction, but of some intellectual conception, mantled on his features. It indicated no pleasure; it betrayed no mirth, nor the anticipation of any enjoyment; but it evinced a profound feeling of satisfaction; for the countenance of this gifted adventurer was transparent to the movements of his mind; and, although few young men were possessed of equal self-command, yet, when his reflections were animated, his countenance could not hide their complexion and character.

After Southennan had concluded the story, there was a short pause, during which Rizzio appeared thoughtful. At last he said slowly, but without hesitation,

" This Count Dufroy is incomprehensible; he hath notions unlike those of other men; he is governed by motives that I cannot understand. He is apt as most men to the frailties of our nature, and yet his mind is not accessible by the influence of any object to which at any time he

seems attached. There is about him an unimpressible probity. He has the ear and the confidence of the Queen: he was the very master of her late husband, Francis. Altogether, he is not a man to be dealt with like others about the Court; for in his courtiership he hath rather impaired than enlarged his estate: and since he came to Scotland, he hath made no endeavour to obtain power, contenting himself with being the friend and personal counsellor of the Queen, in matters purely of private conduct."

" You have given," rejoined Southennan, " a vivid picture of a good great man."

" He is so," said Rizzio; " but I cannot imagine the existence of a man who has not his weaknesses, although I have not yet been able to discover in which of his heels the Count Dufroy is vulnerable."

Southennan looked inquisitively at Rizzio. It struck him as something wonderful, that one who could claim nothing for parentage and but little for advantage of person, should speak of the most accomplished man of the age, and who was no less able than honourable, as if he con-

templated the possibility of reducing him into an agent. He repressed, however, the surprise with which he was so affected, and inquired what Rizzio thought the cause might be, which rendered Dufroy so averse to any mitigation in the unhappy circumstances of Knockwhinnie.

"If," replied Rizzio, "he were a man much addicted to the pageantries of the church, I would say religion; but, being, as he is, a gentleman of free carriage, I must call it honour. Had Knockwhinnie challenged him to open combat, and done him ten times the injury in the lists, it would have been generously forgiven; but the clandestine dagger is, I suspect, the cause that hath made the attack base in his opinion. He accounts, or I am very wrong in my guessing, Knockwhinnie a man naturally prone to take unfair advantages. I have met with some few men like the Count, both in France and Italy, who have stoutly set themselves against self-redressers, and who stand resolutely for the restoration of jurisprudence, which hath so long been hidden in the sepulchres of imperial Rome. These are the leaders of the age, and are doing

that for manners, which your Knoxes and your Luthers and your Calvins, have done, and are doing, for religion."

Southennan started at hearing this: he conceived it was impossible that one trusted with the private correspondence of the Queen, herself so firm in her adherence to the Pope, should hold opinions so pernicious to the cause of the church. But he had no opportunity of making any answer; for at that moment the Count returned from the Queen's apartment.

CHAPTER VIII.

" Know thy own point : this kind, this due degree
Of blindness, weakness, Heaven bestows on thee."
POPE.

Rizzio had observed the effect which his free thought had produced on Southennan, but the Count's entrance deprived him of an opportunity then of extenuating or explaining the sentiments he had expressed. He was conscious that he had said a little more than our hero was ripe for, and that it would be necessary to take some step to regain the ground which he had so inadvertently lost in his good opinion. This induced him somewhat abruptly to retire.

" I have observed of late, Southennan," said Dufroy, as he came towards him, " that Rizzio and you have become great friends. If you can keep your mind independent, and use your ears

and eyes well with him, he will prove a valuable confidant: but take care of yourself."

"How, my Lord? In what way should I take care of myself?"

"Oh!" replied the Count carelessly, "I have perhaps used a wrong term. I only meant to imply that Rizzio is a clever ambitious adventurer, and may be a little lefthanded in his ways of working, by which your natural ingenuousness may be brought into trouble. You were never intended to thrive by Court intrigues."

Southennan replied: "It is odd that Rizzio has just been giving me a description of your Lordship's character, and it was something more flattering than what you have said of him. But I must not tell you, though I account it no breach of confidence to speak of the good opinion one holds of another."

"Then I am honoured," said the Count, "with the good opinion of Rizzio. Verily, if he spoke his true sentiments, it is something to be proud of, for I have never seen a man possessed of such acute perception of character as

that Italian. He enjoys great gifts: his only weakness, and it is one not uncommon to persons of low origin, is to be too sensitive to slights from superiors. This Scottish Court requires a different temperament. The sovereign herself is here not safe from rudeness, and these old Barons, with their wide heaths' and long pedigrees, are not likely to spare Rizzio from the inflictions of their pride. Be you therefore watchful how you become interwoven with his affairs; for depend upon it, he is a man who will make difficulties for himself." And without pausing he added; " and so Knockwhinnie has come again. I have left Adelaide with the Queen, intreating the remission of his outlawry."

" I hope," said Southennan more simply than accorded with his general intelligence, " that your Lordship will not interpose your influence against her suit."

The Count stepped a pace or two backward, and for the space of a minute or so, looked at Southennan with a proud and somewhat stern aspect. Our hero was unconscious of the offence

his words were calculated to give, and appeared in consequence astonished at the effect they had produced. But Dufroy observing him, saw that no offence was intended, and said emphatically,

"He is her father, and I am one of those who hold the ties of nature to be indissoluble even by crime."

"I would she had your advocacy to help her," said Southennan; "the worst deed of Knockwhinnie was his attempt on your life, and it sprung from the offended feelings of a true and loving nature."

"Do you think," said the Count, with some severity," that I am actuated by a resentful remembrance of his attempt."

"How may I answer that, my Lord: it is known only to God and yourself. But, and I trust my frankness will not offend, I have thought your reluctance to mediate for his pardon might be dictated by some sentiment made up of resentment and a sense of wrong."

"I honour your candour, and I trust you will cherish it as the best quality in the mind of

a man in your station," replied the Count. " But I fear Knockwhinnie is one of those violent men who have survived a turbulent age, and are only to be treated as unfit to share in the reciprocities of a better-ordered society. Towards Knockwhinnie, how should it be thought of me that I am ruled by resentment? Have I not made his child my own, when his own rashness caused the forfeiture of his station in the world, and deprived him of the power of protecting her? Had his lady lived, she too could have borne witness how greatly I have endeavoured to appease the anger of her father, who considered her as a deserted wife. Had I been the brother of Knockwhinnie, more I could not have done to disarm the sufferings of those who were dearest to him. But had he been my brother, I would not have looked with less austerity on the contempt of honour and justice, that was in the base guilt of assassination. His attempt, though it failed, was not the less criminal."

The Count delivered these few sentences so earnestly, that Southennan did not venture to

make him any answer, but only acknowledged the high-mindedness of the speaker by a profound and respectful bow. He perceived that the mind of the Count was as Rizzio had described it, inaccessible, at least by the means of ordinary persuasion, and he refrained from further solicitation. He thought, indeed, that it was useless to communicate to a man so lofty and firm of purpose, the wish of Knockwhinnie to be admitted to an interview; and accordingly, after a few short general remarks on indifferent topics, he wished Dufroy good night, and left the Palace.

Southennan had scarcely quitted the gallery, when Chatelard made his appearance. On observing the Count he hesitated to advance, and was on the point of retiring, when several other gentlemen of the household entered, and relieved him from the embarrassment he felt at encountering him alone. Their presence, indeed, so far emboldened him, that he advanced towards Dufroy with as much of his former ease as he could assume; for the rebuff he had met with at the door of the Queen's apartment had

apprised him that his behaviour towards her Majesty had been noticed, and the consciousness of this perplexed him with a diffidence unusual to his character.

The Count, however, received him with his customary urbanity, and adverting to the command which he had been ordered to communicate to those who enjoyed the honour of the Queen's private suppers, led him aside, and with a tone of friendly anxiety, told him, that the order had been given in consequence of his indiscretion.

"It is not," said Dufroy, "commendable in those who receive instances of royal condescension to presume upon them. The favours of princes must not be familiarly accepted; and for a worthy reason, they can only be conferred on a few, and are thereby rare and honourable. Her Majesty's gracious nature, like the light of the day, and the dews of the evening, hath in it an impartial beneficence, an universal quality, that is marred by those who would engross more than their due proportion. I beseech you, Chatelard, to look well to this; for the

bird is often dazzled that flies too much in the sun."

The passion by which the young Frenchman was animated had in it more of desire and ambition than of tenderness. Its promptings were bold and courageous, but the detection of it disturbed his self-possession; still the token he had received of Mary's preference, as he believed it, threw him off his guard, and almost precipitated him, notwithstanding the kindness of the admonishment, to answer the Count frowardly, who, however, before he had time to make any reply, added—

"I see you do not relish my counsel; I can, therefore, only bid you beware. Recollect you are observed, and a rebuke from her Majesty will destroy you."

With these words Dufroy retired, and Chatelard, eying him superciliously as he walked towards the door of the gallery, muttered to himself, with a sneer of scornful bravery—

"Yes; if she does rebuke me!" So much was he already infatuated.

CHAPTER IX.

" Thou shalt be punished for thus frighting me ;
For I am sick, and capable of fears ;
Oppress'd with wrongs, and therefore full of fears ;
A widow, husbandless, subject to fears ;
A woman, naturally born to fears."

SHAKSPEARE.

In the meantime Adelaide had been intreating the Queen for the pardon of her father, with all the earnestness of affection and anxiety. Mary had heard something of his story, and with the gentle compassion of the female heart, she saw not the attempted assassination in those dark hues of guilt with which it appeared to the high and masculine mind of the Count; she was, in consequence, on the point of promising her consent to the reversal of the outlawry, when Dufroy again appeared in her presence.

" This is a sad tale which my poor Adelaide has been telling," said her Majesty to him;

" but as the intention failed, it cannot be consistent with justice to let the law always endure in its rigour against her unfortunate father. What think you ? "

" If the Queen," replied the Count, " desires my opinion, simply as a man, perhaps I should acknowledge the mercifulness of your Majesty's sentiments, especially as I bear no malice against Knockwhinnie; on the contrary, I feel all manner of Christian pity for him. But I have crossed the seas with better purposes than to counsel the remission of offences, which cannot be suffered with impunity, without damaging the frame and cement of society."

Adelaide heard him with sorrow, and clasping her hands, looked imploringly at the Queen, who pensively regarded her for a moment, and then addressed the Count—

" Is not mercy consistent with justice, when the guilty intent has not been performed ? "

Dufroy replied with more than his wonted deference, but with firmness—

" Your Majesty may pardon; and I doubt not the prerogative of mercy is too delicious in

its exercise to your royal nature, to be foregone for the harshness of justice."

Mary regarded him for some time with visible emotion and surprise.

"You then think," said she, "that there may be error in mercy in this case?"

"I do."

The Queen turned her eyes, filled with tears, towards Adelaide, and said, with the softest accents of commiseration,

"Alas! here is a wise and just man, long renowned for his equity and honour; he thinks I may not unblamed comply with your becoming solicitation! Hath not," addressing the Count again, she tenderly subjoined, "Mercy, my Lord, been ever esteemed the gracefullest sister of the virtues? but, if she may not always sit in royal councils, can she be indeed a virtue? This matter touches me with the anguish of exceeding grief. What is the recompense of my abstracted condition, if all show of warmth from others must be rejected, and all kind inclinations repressed in my own bosom? Truly the sovereign of this stormy and inclement realm hath but cold en-

couragement to rule with gentleness. But a few minutes have elapsed since you exhorted me to rebuke the ardour of Chatelard; and what was his offence? He loved not wisely! As if such love were not for its hopelessness more entitled to the charity of pardon, than to be cast into the peril of punishment."

The mildness and the tone of regret with which the Queen expressed herself, alarmed the jealousy of Adelaide, who, in the emotion of the moment, forgot her father. The Count also was surprised; for her Majesty had professed to himself her vexation at the obtrusive freedom with which the infatuated Frenchman sometimes dared to approach her, and had readily assented to the regulation for restricting the admission too freely allowed to her domestic apartments.

"How capricious is woman!" thought he. "Is it possible that the restriction which prudence and dignity equally required, can have produced any interest for that audacity which is too weakly indulged by permitting Chatelard to remain in her service."

But before he could reply the Prior of St. Andrews was announced, whose staid demeanour and sober courtesies had always a serious effect on the Queen; for although he was a person of many virtues, there was yet a collected method in his manner, which, notwithstanding the decided esteem which he was held in by her Majesty, checked the freedom which she allowed to herself with Dufroy and many others. His genius, notwithstanding the defect of his bastardy, awed Mary; and in his presence she felt, as it were, a shadow upon her gaiety. At this particular time, her mind was more moved to melancholy than to mirth; but still his appearance had a saddening and repressing effect, especially when, after stating to her his wish for a private audience, (upon which Dufroy and Adelaide retired) he mentioned with solemnity that he had been requested by the leading Protestant divines, to solicit her Majesty to cause a stricter observance of decorum to be enforced among her household.

" Unseemly brawls," said the Prior, " have taken place at the very portal of the Palace; and

the town is amazed that such tumults should, by any accident, be permitted. During the lifetime of her late Majesty, your royal mother, it was otherwise managed: she was a lady of sedate manners, and, although a stern adversary of the Reformation, yet no one could impute the blemish of any lightness to her deportment. She did more for her faith, by the purity and temperance of her conduct, than by her armies and the arms of France."

The Queen appeared greatly affected, even to distress, by this communication. Tears rushed into her eyes, and she exclaimed, in a tone that partook more of indignation than of sorrow,

"Ah, me! what shall I do? I can stifle and sacrifice my own wishes; but how can I satisfy a people that claim from me a severity which Heaven has been pleased to deny me the power of exercising. In my house there has been no irregularity."

"Alas!" said the Prior, "I beseech you not to deceive yourself with such flattery, for it is rumoured that you evince a favour for the

Frenchman Chatelard, that assorteth not well with your royalty."

" Is it come to that?" cried Mary, roused by an accusation of which her heart acquitted her; " has the young man already made himself such enemies that they so openly desire his ruin?"

" It is not so. It is only your Majesty that is blamed for a carriage towards him unsuitable to your dignity."

The freedom of this speech offended her; her lips became pale, her colour fled, and her eyes sparkled with anger, as she replied,

" James Stuart, forget not the carriage that belongs to yourself! To change in any respect the wonted customs of my house would be to acknowledge they had not been innocent: go and tell those who sent you to rebuke me so, that I will, without their counsel, uphold my dignity; and let them show me more of their duty. Here hath been a poor maiden supplicating a grace for her father, who but only attempted an offence, and I am warned that there may be guilt in granting her petition; then this same Frenchman of whom you speak, hath but offended by

excess of loyalty, and I must forsooth, for to that end such counselling tends, drive him from my service, and put myself under the restraints of a gloomy captivity. Call you this royalty ? Tell me wherein I am a Queen ? Oh ! wherefore did I come to this bleak land of rocks and harder hearts!"

" Hear me, madam," replied the Prior, respectfully; " by duty, and the dearer claim of blood, I entreat your Majesty not to let such words escape you, even in the hearing of these walls !"

" God help me !" cried the Queen, bursting into a flood of tears ; " what shall I do? An orphan ! a widow ! while yet too young to be a wife, almost without a friend ! But I will not thus be schooled ; I have not been the worshipped Queen of France, to bear the unmannerly demands of those that should obey me. That is my answer ;" and with these words she abruptly retired into an inner chamber.

CHAPTER X.

"O place and greatness, millions of false eyes
Are stuck upon thee! volumes of report
Run with these false and most contrarious guesses
Upon thy doings! thousand 'scapes of wit
Make thee the father of their idle dream,
And rack thee in their fancies."

SHAKSPEARE.

The Prior of St. Andrew's had not long retired, when the Abbot of Kilwinning, attended by Father Jerome, came to beg an audience of the Queen, and were at once admitted. It was evident to them, that she had been recently agitated; the traces of distress were visible on her countenance, and there was an air of dejection in her appearance, which rendered her more interesting than when her beauty was unclouded.

"Madam," said the Abbot, approaching to-

wards her, " I fear the errand I am come upon will not be acceptable to your Majesty."

" Then," replied the Queen dejectedly, " come with it to-morrow; for in truth I am very sad. I have had enough of such errands to-night. But I must endure my lot. Alas! it promised once to be a brighter and happier."

Father Jerome softly whispered to the Abbot, reminding him that their business was urgent, and the Queen, partly over-hearing him, subjoined,

" But if the matter presses, I am ready to hear it."

The Abbot then briefly recapitulated Knockwhinnie's story, which had been so recently related to her, and she exclaimed impatiently,

" All this I know; but what can I do in it?"

" The unhappy man has been this evening taken," said the Abbot, " and is now in the custody of the city officers: his offence is less than it seemed, for the blow which he aimed at the Count Dufroy was intended for another."

" How doth that lighten his guilt? It rather magnifies it; seeing that in his rashness he attempted the life of one that was blameless."

"Even so," replied the Abbot; "but he had such provocation that justice almost warranted his intention. The man who did him the wrong is also in custody, and hath acknowledged his guilt."

"But Father Abbot, how comes it that you are moving in this business?"

The Abbot in reply informed the Queen, that Southennan had urged him on behalf of Knockwhinne to solicit the reversal of the outlawry.

"My aged brother here," said he, "is of his household, and your Majesty hath not in all the west country a better subject than Southennan; nor the church a truer son. He sent at this late hour to beg my mediation, with strong assurances of faithful service could the boon be obtained."

"Southennan!" said the Queen; "is it the same that is so often here? Ah now I know the motive of his visits, Adelaide. Good Father Abbot, I am much inclined to compassionate the unfortunate Knockwhinnie: but I fear he must go first to trial. I may not unblamed,

until he hath passed the ordeal, grant him grace. I am still too young in this land to venture on any measure which may not accord with the rude temper of the people. There has been much preaching among them of late, as I am told, concerning the impunity allowed to breaches of the law, and the self-revenging of private wrongs. It hath scared the mercy-dove from off the sceptre. But what I may do without offending justice, shall be done, were it only to help the suit of Southennan with my gentle Adelaide, and win from her for him some portion of that regard which she throws away on Chatelard."

The Abbot and Father Jerome at these words exchanged significant looks, which the Queen sharply observing, said,

" And has the story spread to you ? "

" I crave pardon, Madam," said the Abbot, " but it is my duty to report, that this night it has been said that Chatelard was distinguished by some signal act of your royal favour."

" 'Tis false."

" We," said the Abbot thoughtfully, " the true and ancient brethren of the church, account

it an invention of the heretics to blemish your Majesty in the eyes of your people, whom they drive and devour as they list, like wolves among sheep."

"It argues," replied the Queen with emphasis, "more honour in the professors of our faith to discredit such baleful slanders. There can be no rectitude in the minds of those who propagate such injuries. It is to them I owe the malice that hath environed my throne with so many fears and menaces."

"Your Majesty speaks great truth," replied the Abbot; "but things so troubled as they are at present cannot long remain so. The divisions that were amongst us are healing, and by your countenance we hope to see the Church again uplift her banner in Scotland as high as it ever waved before. She is but as the sun labouring with eclipse; the darkness which intercepts her light must soon pass."

"Would it may be so," said the Queen; "but those unhozzled spirits, that work in darkness, grow daily bolder; and all the signs of the times augur success to them."

"It must be so, whilst there is no manly will to govern our endeavours. The Prior of St. Andrew's, who is so near of kin to your Majesty, hath openly espoused the cause of the schismatics, and they reckon on his favour with your Majesty, for great things."

"They shall be taught better; they meddle too much with what concerns me. But I am only a weak and inexperienced woman!" said the Queen.

"Yes;" replied the Abbot, echoing the sadness in the tone of her last expression, "and therein we plainly discern where our cause is most infirm. Would I might venture to tell your Majesty freely what we dread and what we think?"

"Let me hear it," cried the Queen; "my heart is open to all petitions, and my ears are greedy of advice."

The Abbot, after a short pause, said with great apparent humility.

"It hath been a suggestion amongst us, to pray your Majesty to lighten your cares by dividing them with a consort."

"Verily," said the Queen, with a smile, "this is not the season for match-making. We are still too much in the blast and shower: the mating time is only in the spring days, when boughs are budding and meadows green. But the night is far advanced; I pray you, therefore, Father Abbot, to come betimes in the morning, and the matter of your errand shall then be duly considered; meantime, let me be remembered in your orisons."

The Abbot and Father Jerome retired, and as they were passing down the gallery, Rizzio met them. The Abbot waved his hand to Father Jerome, who walked on to the stairs, where Baldy was waiting to assist him home. It was evident that some recent intercourse had taken place between the Abbot and Rizzio; who addressed him with a degree of freedom, as if he felt himself on some equality with that dignitary.

"Well," said Rizzio, "what success, my Lord?"

"She is in some distress; and hath already, contrary to her inclination, been tampered with against Knockwhinnie."

"But," said Rizzio, "did you hint what is said of Chatelard?"

"As much as was becoming. She had been fretted by it before our audience; but something in her humour, which was ready to flame up, indicated that whatever had been told her, had only served to kindle her resentment."

"Indeed!" said Rizzio, thoughtfully; "Did you allude to marriage?"

"I did but allude. She was not in a mood to listen to me; she spoke dejectedly of the unhappy condition of the kingdom."

"Will she, think you," inquired Rizzio, "still retain Chatelard, after being so much admonished for the distinction with which she has treated him, and on which he so much presumes."

"Has others then," said the Abbot, "been counselling her on his imprudence; there must have been. But if her will be in it, admonition may be spared; she hath the headiness of her race, and will take her own way. I am, however, to be again with her in the morning, when I pray St. Mary's help that she may be in a more composed frame!"

The Abbot then parted from him, and Rizzio walked slowly up the gallery. At the farther end he paused for a short time, and then turning round advanced two or three paces, when he halted, and fixing his eyes on the ground, ruminated to the following effect;—

" I am like Cæsar when he passed the Rubicon—the report of her favour shown to Chatelard, has determined my course and fate—the tale cannot be recalled—it has had wings—spread like an epidemic. I am alarmed at the speed with which it has infected all sorts of the world, the reformed and unreformed—the good, the bad, the foolish, and the wise—all cry out at her unworthy condescension. Some say there is no bar in the law of Scotland, by which she may not raise him even to sit beside her;—he has been of late reserved—averse to me, as if he feared some hindrance from me; and he shall too. A shallow talking Frenchman, that hath as little matter in his mind, as there is substance in the rainbow! but I must be wary. The quick infection with which the story hath rushed all abroad, warns me to be wary. Yes; the mar-

riage is the thing.—Where shall a fool be found, ductile enough to bend to those who may promote him; fool, indeed, must the husband be of this Queen of rebels, for no better are these irascible Scots. That is, however, a thing not ripe for action—something bolder on the part of Chatelard must yet be done, and to help it forward be my first business."

CHAPTER XI.

> " Oh, how wretched !
> Is the poor man that hangs on princes' favours :
> There is betwixt that smile we would aspire to,
> That sweet aspect of princes, and their ruin,
> More pangs and fears than wars or women have."
>
> HENRY VIII.

WE hope our worthy readers have sagacity enough to discern that, during the transactions in Holyrood House, Knockwhinnie had been taken before the magistrates, where he had given such an account of himself, that it had been deemed necessary to call Southennan before them, and that, as we have described, Auchenbrae was carried with him and surrendered.

The delinquents were both ordered to be held in custody for trial; and our hero, seeing no other way of assisting the father of Adelaide,

determined, in consequence, to seek the mediation of some of the ecclesiastical dignitaries with the Queen. He accordingly returned to his lodgings, and dispatched Father Jerome to entreat the good offices of the Abbot of Kilwinning. The result has been related.

Early next morning Southennan went to the Palace, for the purpose of again trying his influence with Count Dufroy, and also of consulting Rizzio. On approaching the portal he met Chatelard, and recollecting what Rizzio had told him of the disposition which the Queen had evinced towards him, he resolved to try what agency he might obtain in him, to second the solicitation for the pardon of Knockwhinnie.

Chatelard was at the time walking towards the gardens; Southennan immediately joined him, and after the compliments of the morning, opened his business by saying—

" It has been observed by all the Court, Chatelard—indeed, you have made no secret of it yourself—how much you are attached to Adelaide."

Whether there was any thing intentionally

ironical in the manner with which our hero expressed himself, or that Chatelard, conscious of his artifice, felt it as such, is not for us to determine; but he reddened and appeared disturbed, which Southennan observing, quieted his apprehensions by adding—

"But whatever may be your sentiments respecting Adelaide, I have to entreat your aid and service in a matter that deeply concerns her peace of mind, and is very interesting to myself. You are aware of the unfortunate condition of her father?"

Chatelard, having by this time recovered his self-possession, vehemently declared how happy he should be to render even the smallest service to the lady, and his desire to be useful in any degree to one whom he so much esteemed as Southennan.

"I doubt not your good-will," replied our hero; "had I not indeed had confidence in it, I should not have ventured to solicit the favour I now wish you to do for both. The Count Dufroy has, in a manner which prevents me from applying to him again, declined to entreat

the Queen, on behalf of Knockwhinnie, and last night, at my very earnest suit the Lord Abbot of Kilwinning, undertook, without success, to move the Queen's grace to grant a pardon."

"And would you," said Chatelard, with a smile, and something like exultation in his manner, "expect me to succeed, where Dufroy deems his interference would be in vain, and so great a man as the Lord Abbot has failed?"

"It has not been exactly so," said Southennan. "The Count refuses, not from any question as to the efficacy of his influence, but because he regards the offence of Knockwhinnie as one of those which, for the public safety, should be punished. Moreover, I am informed by my chaplain, who went with the Abbot to the Queen, that her Majesty hath not absolutely denied the pardon. I have therefore thought, as she permits to you the privilege of addressing her more freely than any other of her attendants, you might find an opportunity of seconding the application of Adelaide."

"I can with sincerity promise you to do all

that I may have it in my power to do; but you are aware, from what took place last night, that the Queen is hereafter only to be accessible upon request or summons. Now I doubt if it might not be to offend men of such weight as the Count and the Abbot, were I openly to work in this business."

" Nay," said Southennan, " it matters not how you work after your promise: and surely it can never be deemed culpable to be a little zealous in the cause of humanity."

Chatelard appeared for a few seconds to ruminate, and then he asked, if Adelaide could not obtain a private interview for him with the Queen.

The inquiry startled Southennan: it implied a degree of boldness which seemed to provoke hazard. It was an intrigue of so delicate a kind, that he said—

" Would it not seem more consistent with your attachment to Adelaide to offer your service, and by that obtain her assistance. I stand not so fair in her opinion as to offer a suggestion which would come with so much more grace

and effect from you. Can you doubt that, showing so much interest for her father, you will not recommend yourself to her affection."

This again touched the tender secret of Chatelard, and he blushed, and was confused; but, recovering himself, he rejoined briskly,

" In sooth, Southennan, I will do my best in the business; but when, or how, must depend upon fortune."

While they were holding this conversation, the Abbot of Kilwinning, agreeably to his appointment, was admitted to an audience of the Queen; whom he found, as he had anticipated, in a more serene mood than that in which he had left her the preceding evening.

" I have," said her Majesty, " thought well of your application, and I have consulted the Chancellor, who speaks wisely, as I think, on the matter. We shall let Knockwhinnie abide his trial; he may be acquitted on it: but should the result be otherwise, then, without detriment to the motives of our royal mercy, a pardon may be extended, and reason shown wherefore it is granted."

The Abbot commended the discretion of her Majesty; observing, however, that there might be more risk in the consequences of such proceedings on the opinion of the people, than were the affair quietly passed over; "For," said he, "Knockwhinnie is firm to his faith, and should he be found guilty, and afterwards pardoned, there are not wanting tongues who will despitefully impugn the motives of your Majesty's leniency."

Mary acknowledged that she saw the difficulties and the hardships to which she was exposed, and said,

"Would I had not consulted the Chancellor! because, having assented to his advice, I cannot unblamed recede."

"And yet," replied the Abbot, "there cannot be much wrong in doing so; for the Chancellor in substance agrees with the merciful inclinations of your Majesty. In the diseased condition of the time, it were better to pursue the expedient rather than the legal course. The offence of Knockwhinnie happened years ago; it is almost forgotten, but a trial will revive the popular re-

sentment which the deed at first excited. Your Majesty cannot afford to tantalize the rabid public."

"There is good counsel, Father Abbot," replied the Queen pensively, "in what you say. And will it not be thought that my poor Adelaide has obtained from me the pardon?"

"The people may be so taught," said the Abbot.

The Queen made no answer for some time; at last she said, "Might it not be as well for me to consult the Prior of St. Andrews? He hath always shown himself most anxious to save me from the peril of doing wrong."

"In that," replied the Abbot, "I would not presume to control your Majesty's inclinations; but he hath leagued himself with the enemies of our holy cause."

The Queen relapsed into her rumination, and after a considerable pause, during which she played with the fingers of her right hand on the table as on a virginal, and her eyes were vacant and abstracted, she rose, and with a graceful and benign smile said,

"I do not promise to take your advice; but I will think of it, with the wish that mercy may be reconciled with justice in adopting it. This matter, my Lord Abbot, hath within a short time given me much trouble. If by granting the pardon the vexations can be ended, be assured I lack no counselling to quench them. Rest with this assurance; and in the course of the day you shall hear of what I can do."

The Abbot, bowing over her hand, retired without making any reply.

CHAPTER XII.

" —— Well! Heaven's above all; and there be souls that must be saved, and there be souls must not be saved."

OTHELLO.

The news of Knockwhinnie's arrest and of Auchinbrae's surrender, were the topics of the morning among the guests of the Unicorn.— Cornylees had, for some cause or another, been the previous night sorning about the wynds and closses in the neighbourhood of the Cowgate, according to the use and wont of the west country Lairds when they visit Edinburgh; and in the course of his nocturnal adventures had heard of the hunt of Auchinbrae by Johnnie Gaff, and the other adventures of the night. These he was reporting with his accustomed glee to the guests at the breakfast-table, and the Maister Balwham,

who was in attendance, hearing that Knockwhinnie had been taken, flung his towel over his shoulder, and putting in his little round head from behind to the ear of Cornylees, said, in a whisper,

"Oh, dear! but that's sair news; when ye hae done wi' your bit kipper, I would treat you wi' a stoup o' the best o't in my ain cham'er. Puir Knockwhinnie was, in the days of his rectitude, often a gude customer to the Unicorn, and it behoves me, as the host and maister thereof, to lighten his captivity. And I dinna ken, when a man's back's to the wa', ane mair able to help him than yoursel', Cornylees."

The promise of the stoup of wine spurred the appetite of the Laird, and he made more than common speed with his kipper; and then, wiping his mouth and hands, rose from table. The Maister Balwham at the same time, laying down his towel and taking off his apron, as he always did on occasions when he gave what he called "a gratis" to a friend, walked with Cornylees into his own room.

"Now," said he, "sit ye down, Laird, and

and bide till I get a candle to look in the far neuk o' the cellar, where I'll maybe be able to muddle out a flask o' the right sort."

"Atweel, gudeman, I'se warrant I hae been guilty o' waur in my time, in course now."

The Maister Balwham then left him, and presently returned with a flask and two Venetian goblets, which he placed on the table, and seated himself at it opposite to Cornylees. He then untied the bit of leather from the mouth of the flask—in those days the substitute for corks—and filling the two goblets, said,

"Now, Laird, before I speak my mind, here's as gude a bribe for gude-will as ever was slippit in the shape o' gold into the loof o' a Lord o' the Parliament. Pree 't; isna' that prime? Many's the time that Knockwhinnie—hech, but he was a blithe lad!—has called this nectar; aye, and tried to giet even a better name, when his tongue had lost the power o' utterance. Puir man! dinna' ye think that it would be a comfort to his cauld heart, in yon gruesome cage o' bolts and bars, if he had a tasting o't?"

Cornylees having drank off his glass, and smacked his lips, gave his host a knowing wink, and said,

"Balwham, that 'll do! Weel, I maun allow that Knockwhinnie is a gude judge o' wine, in course now. Really this is *rosa solus!*" And he held out his glass to be filled again.

Balwham, in filling the glass, said,

"I wonder if there's a possibility o' doing a service to the disjasket gentleman. I would gie you, Cornylees, a flask o' this to your dinner free gratis, if ye could help me in a kind matter."

The Laird professed his willingness to do any thing for any gentlemen in straits, even without reward: "But really, Balwham," said he, "the very smell o' this cordial, in course now, would prick a man on to an adventure better than the rowels o' his spurs. What would ye hae me to do?"

"Weel, Laird," replied Balwham, "I'll no' be blate. I saw, frae the first day ye dieted in the Unicorn, that ye were o' a generous nature, and fond o' gude drink, sae I'll speak out.

Could ye, in a sympatheezing manner, gang up to the Tolbooth, and speer for ane Johnnie Gaff, a decent bodie that speaks Latin, and get him by hook or crook; even ye may gang the length o' a palmy wi' him, and I'll thole the cost—to let you see your auld frien', ye understand, Knockwhinnie!—and tell the winsom gentleman how I'm ready to do a turn for him, and that the best in a' the Unicorn is at his command."

"In course now, I'll willingly do that; but this wine, I see, will no' bide in the bicker."

Balwham poured out another bumper to the Laird; but having the fear of his business before his eyes, he only gave himself a small drop, which Cornylees saw with delight, as it was an assurance that the remainder of the flask was destined for him.

"In course now, Unicorn, I'll no' be backward in my errand; but dinna' ye think it would be kindly if I took a flask or twa up in my pouch? Ye ken, if I getna' a visibility o' the prisoner, in course now, Johnnie Gaff can tak' the wine intil him."

"'Deed," replied the Maister Balwham, "that's a friendly thought; and surely I'll no' let you gang toom-handed to yon dungeon o' dolorosity."

The Laird, taking hold of the flask by the neck, said,

"In course now, Balwham, ye're at your last dribble; but I'll no' let this wine grow dead; it's o'er gude to be lost. In course now, being auld, it canna' be strong."

"I wouldna' trust it, Laird; but you west country folk hae baith big bellies and strong heads; sae ye may take your will o't."

"In course now," replied the Laird, beginning to give ocular demonstration in contradiction of his own axiom, "that age did not always imply the lack of strength, especially in wine."

"But, Laird," said the host of the Unicorn, "dinna' ye think it would be as weel to leave what's in the flask, till ye come back, for it's a stay brae frae this to the Tolbooth, and ye'll be nane the waur o' a drappie when ye come back."

"By my Lord, auld Unicorn! we'll hae then a fresh bottle. In course now," taking another glass—" here's leil hearts and gude wine."

"Weel, weel, that's a blithe Laird! Just gang awa', for ye ken my business disna' allow me to clishmaclaver. I hear customers in the house. Coming, gentlemen," and with these words he whisked out of the room; and Cornylees, with a blouzy countenance, made the best of his way towards the Tolbooth, where he had no difficulty in finding Johnnie Gaff.

Johnnie looked at him somewhat suspiciously, and turning round to one of the other halberderdiers, touched his own forehead to signify that he was aware of the Laird's condition and added—" But *in vino veritas*, he can do nae harm."

Then addressing the Laird he inquired whom he wanted; and Cornylees made him understand, that he had brought a flask of wine from the Unicorn for a friend of the host's.

"Weel, I'll do any thing, in a ceevil way, to oblige the Maister Balwham, for there's no a

publican in the burgh o' Embro that has sic a *ne plus ultra* o' discretion. Ye see what it's to hae a frien' in Court, Sir."

" By my Lord!" exclaimed the Laird, putting his hand in his pocket, and giving Johnnie a piece of money from his purse, he added, as well as his subsiding intelligibility would allow him—" Ye're an honest fellow, in course now, and kens what's what?"

Johnnie, putting the money into his pocket, took him under the arm and helped him to the foot of the stair, where calling for Lockie, he desired him to allow the gentleman, " as he has been discreet, to hae twa words with ane o' the prisoners."

The Laird, as he clambered up the stair behind the gaoler, said—

" In course now, amang your blackbirds ye hae gotten my auld friend Montgomery o' Auchenbrae, in your cage yestreen. Hech, but it's pitifu' to think o' the changes that befa' gude auld families. His father was a worthy man, and left twa bolls, twa firlots, twa pecks, and twa lippies yearly frae the lands o' Capel-

rig to the monks o' the Abbacy o' Paisley for his soul's health!"

Here the remembrance of such benevolence and piety came softly over the Laird's heart, and he began to weep.

"Ah!" continued he, "but sic things are a' gane bye now; souls and bodies are laid in the kirkyard as if they were clods o' the valley. Oh, what'll become o' us, if, after a' this straemash that has been in the land, there should be a purgatory!"

Led by this to suppose it was Auchenbrae whom the Laird desired to see, and being come to the room where he was confined, Lockie opened the door, gave him admission, and having locked him in, went down to the ward-room, where the halberdiers were sitting.

"*Tempus fugy!*" cried Johnnie, starting up as he saw him. "I'll break the back o' this groat amang us. Marion Bickers has had a noble browst. Come, it'll just gie ilk a chappin and leave a bodle to the lassie."

Johnnie, accordingly, leading the way, fol-

lowed by the other halberdiers, " all being forefoughten and exhoust," adjourned to the kitchen of Marion Bickers, where a tappit hen was ordered of her last brewing, *pro bono publico.*

CHAPTER XIII.

"For well you know this is a pitiful case."
SHAKSPEARE.

PUNISHMENT, whether well or ill deserved, has always an unpleasant effect on the mind and temper of those who are obliged to endure it. Auchenbrae had scarcely been taken before the magistrates when his virtuous resolutions began to supple, and his high-mindedness to ebb. Before he was a couple of hours locked up in his dungeon, nothing remained of all the regrets and griefs which had hovered in his spirit as he sat alone in the twilight on the top of Arthur's Seat. Like the golden clouds of the evening, they had melted away, and were succeeded by the gloom of guilty desires, and he almost gnawed his hands with rage at his own

folly in giving himself up so weakly to justice. But he still trusted, that by the powerful influence of his family he would be allowed to commute the penalties of the law. Instead, therefore, of being in any thing like a penitential mood when Cornylees broke in upon him, his mind was writhing with the spasms of vindictive thought. Not conceiving that his solitude was to be disturbed by a companion, and believing Cornylees to be another prisoner, he rushed upon him fiercely before he was well within the door, and shook him, as it were, with the wrath and worrying of a mastiff, demanding to know why he was so obtruded upon.

The Laird recognized his voice, and still continuing his maudlin interjections, said—

" Hech! Auchenbrae; but I'm wae for you; I'm very wae, in course now; I'm wae for your father's son: oh, but I'm wae!"

Auchenbrae knew his voice and flung him off, saying—

" And what the devil has brought you here, Cornylees?"

" In course now, I'll tell you: but oh, this is

a black job. Alack! alack! in course now, I canna' help greeting: but it wasna' you, Auchenbrae, that I came to sing wally-wally wi!" and stumbling along the floor he fell upon the truckle-bed in the corner.

Auchenbrae regarded him with something of disgust when he saw how utterly incapable he was of assisting himself, and returned towards the narrow grated window which looked up towards the castle.

" But in course now, I forgot the wine," said Cornylees; and he laughed, or rather yelled, at his negligence, as he lay on the bed. Then he cried, resuming his maudlin tone, " Puir Auchenbrae, the puir birdie that was catched in a girn, and is now in a cage!"

By these exclamations the prisoner discovered that he was only a visitor, and seeing his helpless condition, at once determined to turn it to his own advantage. Accordingly, he immediately began to pull off his jerkin, and to say that he was grieved to see his old friend so very unwell, advising him to undress, as he would be much better in bed. Cornylees dolorously

assented to all that was proposed, and was presently stript of his apparel, and before the operation was completed he was fast asleep. Auchenbrae lost no time in doffing his own and donning the garb of his friend, determined to watch the return of the gaoler; for which purpose he armed himself with a bar wrenched from the grate.

In due time Robin Lockie returned, considerably elated by his share of the potations; indeed he was in such a wavering condition when he looked in to bid the visitor come forth, that Auchenbrae had no occasion to use his weapon: on the contrary, he only pulled him in and threw him down beside the Laird, springing out at the same moment, and turning the key. He then stepped softly down the stair, lest any of the halberdiers should be on guard at the foot: nor was this a weak fear, for Johnnie Gaff was there, *in propria persona*, holding firmly by his halberd, and swinging too and fro, like a tree in the wind, with the effects of Cornylees' largess.

Auchenbrae paused to consider what he ought

to do in such jeopardy, when he heard a rustling above, and the voice of Robin Lockie, crying to get out. Not a moment was to be lost. Johnnie Gaff too heard the alarm, and was turning round as well as he could, when the fugitive pushed him down with all his strength, and leaped over him as he lay sprawling in the street.

The land, in which Mistress Marjory's house was the ninth story, stood in one of the wynds near to the Luckenbooths, and Auchenbrae escaped into it undiscovered. He ascended the nine stairs with more than his wonted agility, and beat on the door for admission, a peal that would have deafened the knocking of the biggest iron knocker that hangs from the mouth of the fiercest lion's head that frowns on a footman.

Hughoc heard the sound, and being the nimblest in the house, opened the door. Auchenbrae bolted in, and without saying a word, rushed into Mistress Marjory's bed-chamber, where he instantly began to denude himself of Cornylees' habiliments. The boy recognised him

at once, and the uproar in the house at such an invasion, was shrill and hoarse and vehement. Baldy, Father Jerome, Mistress Marjory, and her hand-maid, came forth to see the cause and occasion of the disturbance.— Hughoc did not mingle in the fray; but knowing it was near the time when his master would expect him at the Unicorn, where he regularly dined, ran off, primed with the news of this new adventure.

In the meantime the noise of the imprisoned jailor had continued with unabated violence. and had awakened Cornylees, while the fumes of the sherries were still clouding his brain. " In what direction has he fled?" was the universal cry; and in all directions the halberdiers ran for a short time in pursuit of the fugitive: it was in vain.

In the interim our host of the Unicorn had become uneasy; he knew the magic that was in his wine, and had seen it taking effect. He feared that it would master the discretion of Cornylees, and that he would himself be brought into trouble. This induced him to come

up, in the short interval while his dinner guests were assembling, from the Canongate, to see what had happened at the Tolbooth, and he reached the door of the ward-room in the moment of alarm.

Johnny Gaff, on seeing him, pounced upon him like a hawk upon its quarry, crying,

" Here's a *soshy criminy !* Ye scoundrel Balwham, would ye take the bread out o' my mouth ? "

" Whist, whist, Johnnie ! there's been a mistake ! Hech ! but I'm in a flurry, and our gentlemen will be wud if I'm no at my post. Just, Johnnie my man, slip in wi' me, and I'll tell you a' about it. Ae Laird is just as good for a prisoner as anither !"

Johnnie holding him by the lapel of his jerkin, took him into the ward-house, and said—

" If I didna ken, Balwham, that ye were an honest man, I would make an example o' you *in modum peny.*"

" Hout tout, Johnnie ! speak mair like yoursel' ! Knockwhinnie ye ken, your auld maister, was a true friend o' mine. I'm sure ye canna'

hae forgotten the sprees he used to hae in the Unicorn, before he first gaed to France; could I hear o' his being in a dolefu' prison, and no do something to cheer him? Sae thinking Cornylees was just the man to do the turn for me, I solaced him wi' a flask o' our best, to gang and see Knockwhinnie; but the wine proving right stuff, it ran awa' wi' the heels o' his understanding; and that's the even-down truth. But, if ye'll take my advice, ye'll keep your thumb on the whole affair, and ne'er let on, but that Auchinbrae is still in the Tolbooth. It can mak nae difference to the likes o' Cornylees to keep him safe for twa or three days!"

"Wrangeous imprisonment, Mr. Balwham, what may come o'er me for that?"

"Poh! poh! my man Johnnie, we'll souther a' right wi' anither flask. At any rate thraw the key upon him for this day; and come ye down to the house belyve in the gloaming, and I'll gie you sic a caulker o' Nantz as will gar your eyne stand wet-shod in your head!"

Johnnie, who was still in the mists of Luckie Bicker's brewing, thought the proposition not

unreasonable : so, after some farther discourse, the host of the Unicorn was permitted to return in time to give his wonted tendance on his guests.

CHAPTER XIV.

" Be it as you shall privately determine.
Th' affair cries haste, and speed must answer."
OTHELLO.

THE agitation which intentions of guilt produce in their conception, comes of the rough handling with which the Devil eagerly grasps the chain of destiny, to drag the fated to their doom. It was so with Rizzio who, after his interview with the Abbot of Kilwinning, when he had retired from the gallery to his own chamber for the night, was overwhelmed with compunctuous self-remonstrances. Alas! they only showed how firmly the Adversary had made good his hold. For he deplored not the dangers to which his machinations would expose Chatelard; his prophetic remorse was all of the hazards that might involve himself; and

the occasional fits of resolution to proceed no further in the business partook, in consequence, more of dread than of contrition. But in the morning this qualm of morality had left him, and he resumed the intents and purposes of ambition with refreshed courage.

He knew that Chatelard regularly walked early in the gardens, to which he himself occasionally resorted at the same hour: but it was not with him so much a custom; nor indeed did method often appear in his actions, for it was a part of his system to be seemingly actuated by impulses, in order to obtain impunity from remark when he might happen to require it.

It were needless, therefore, to conjecture whether from design or purpose he chanced this morning to be in the gardens first, but he was there some time before the young Frenchman made his appearance: other gallants of the Court were, however, walking in the parterre, but he avoided them. The weather, indeed, was dull and anti-social in all its influences. A heavy grey mist rested on Arthur's

Seat, and hung in masses along the front of Salisbury Craigs. The air was calm, and the smoke of the city stood erect on the chimney tops, like trees incrusted with hoar frost among the huge rocks of shattered mountains. The shrubs in the gardens were depressed with the last dews of the summer; for the bright season was now over, and the dejected flowers were weeping to overflowing, as if affected with some moral sentiment of sorrow; not a chirp of bird or insect was heard save the hum of the bee, and it was sympathetic to yawning; a number of maidens were bleaching their new-washed clothes on the margin of the rill that flows in the meadow; but neither lilt nor laugh was heard from them; nor was jest or good-morrow exchanged with the briskest galliard that passed on the footpath beside them. The slow spirit of a soberness almost sullen, touched as it were with torpor the springs of thought, and obscured the vision of the mind.

The effect on Rizzio, knit up as he was with stern purposes, was something like induration,

insomuch that when Chatelard joined him he seemed almost repulsive.

" You look," said the Frenchman approaching, " as if this grey-mantled morning had displeased you."

" It must be so," was the reply; " and yet I have some cause for heaviness. I would, for the Queen's sake, this affair of Knockwhinnie was quietly disposed of; considering your openly professed affection for Adelaide, it surprises many that you take so little interest in it. Be assured, Chatelard, that such remissness makes some suspect the sincerity of your professions."

The Italian, in saying so, threw at him one of those deep-searching glances of his vivid eye which few could withstand, and perceiving that Chatelard felt the whole force of the insinuation, he added, with well-assumed carelessness, but with another look that proved how little it was so—

" It has been expected that by this time you would have employed your influence with the Queen."

" Influence! what influence can I have with

her Majesty; yesterday Southennan talked to the same effect. How is it supposed that I have any influence?"

Rizzio darted at him one of his most penetrating glances, and hastily looking around to see that no one was near, said in a low impressive voice—

" It has been observed that the Queen, of late, takes much pleasure in your music, and honours you with particular condescension."

" I am not conscious of receiving such favour," replied Chatelard, blushing, and turning aside to conceal his emotion.

" Come, come, my friend," rejoined the dark discerning Italian, in a free confidential manner. " It is not to be disguised; the whole Court have observed it:" and sinking his voice, he said significantly, " some bright change is expected."

" What change?" inquired Chatelard, with a throbbing heart.

" That the aurelia, still so insensible, shall soon be in motion, moving upwards; and anon on wing, and happy in the radiance of the sun."

"Would you have me swallow such a philter? I thought, Rizzio, you had a better opinion of my understanding."

"Nay, I did not say you were so weak as to love beyond loyalty; moreover, your heart is pledged to Adelaide, so you have freely confessed, no doubt to warn all of the Court from rivalry. Nor can it be imputed to you as a fault if the Queen——it would be too bold to say what I might, but there are few so likely as yourself to win favour in a lady's eye."

The agitation and confusion of Chatelard were extreme during this speech, which was delivered with all the craft of Rizzio, and with such illustrations in his looks and accents as would have left no cloud upon its meaning had it been less plainly expressed.

"Had this been said, Rizzio," replied Chatelard, recovering his self-possession, "at a drenched table, and in the presence of boon companions and flowing flasks, I might have answered you in a strain befitting the vanity of your suggestions; but here, in this cool morning, amidst the universal freshness of flowers and

dewy leaves, it is so much at variance with propriety that I am puzzled how it should be considered."

" Be wary," replied the Italian, calmly and collectedly; " we are in this country both strangers, something we have known of each other, and that good fortune is the patron on whom we both chiefly rely. I pray you therefore, to have some confidence in me. I do not ask you to tell me what it may be prudent to conceal, but by your conduct I shall guess if you understand me. It is manifest, though it may not be seen nor be thought of by those whom you have taken such pains to persuade you are enamoured of Adelaide, that——"

" What?" exclaimed Chatelard, panting with emotion.

" You love her not, not more than you do one of those roses which blush in your admiration! Chatelard, whether you give or refuse me your confidence, I will tell you that your loquacious fondness—as if love were ever else than dreamy, still, and meditative!—has not deceived me. It is a mask. In the name of

friendship be not offended with my frankness; but leaving that and all other controversies, it may serve you to intercede for the father of Adelaide with the Queen. It hath already caused surprise that you take no part in a suit which all the household are so earnest in. Come what may of it, whether to gain thanks from Adelaide, or from Adelaide's father, or, let me say it in your ear, to sound the Queen's bosom, it is a task that may not be delayed."

And so saying, without waiting for an answer, he parted from him, and returned into the Palace.

CHAPTER XV.

"For 'tis most easy
The inclining Desdemona to subdue
In any honest suit."
OTHELLO.

THE Queen, after her interview with the Abbot of Kilwinning, passed an ill-omened night. The demon of the troubled time visited both her waking thoughts and her dreams. She was also grieved for Adelaide, and felt an obscure boding of sorrow coming to herself. Her couch was in consequence uneasy; and when the grey morning looked in at her lattice, it seemed like the visage of a widow. The day was indeed widowed of the sun.

She rose at an unwonted hour, unrefreshed and dejected, with an intention of sending for Adelaide to accompany her into the gardens;

but the unhappy night which she had herself spent, induced her to prefer, on this occasion, the Lady Mary Livingstone, who was of a gayer nature, and much better calculated to dissipate the hazy griefs which dimmed her spirit.

They descended into the garden soon after Rizzio had left it; and while Chatelard was musing on the advice, which even to him appeared bold and strange, they approached towards the walk along which he was slowly and musingly moving.

Mary Livingstone directed the Queen's attention towards him, and remarked that he too seemed to have been molested in his sleep; adding, " Doubtless, partly from the same cause which darkened your Majesty's dreams. In sooth, I should account his love but light, if he felt not for me, were I Adelaide."

" Ah!" replied the Queen, " is it not truly so? Alas, poor Adelaide! I doubt the love burns but in one heart. It has sometimes seemed to me as if he felt peevishly under the beam of her too evident attachment."

" He is a froward and unsteady varlet," re-

plied Mary Livingstone. " Beshrew me! were Adelaide to take my counsel, he should feel that I could resent it; especially as Southennan, who is the properest man of the two, would lay his neck under her heel for the tithe of half the beneficence she is wasting on that effigy of a lover —reality he cannot be, to talk so loudly of his love, and yet never vouchsafe one private whisper to warrant its sincerity."

"Yet," said the Queen, "he is not one of those blushing youths that would die at a frown. I think in all my experience, even in France, where men are not too much afflicted with bashfulness, I have not met a gallant with more levity in his eye: he often disturbs me. Verily, I must find out a way to repress his bravery, or lose his servitude, which I cannot well spare, both on account of his clerkship and his music. He is truly exquisite on the lute; and I would have him oftener when my spirits are sad, and need soothing, but that he grows too bold and familiar."

"Your Majesty has a lively discernment: we simple maidens of the anti-chamber have

not, however, detected such ventures about him. He is as docile as grimalkin, and as capricious as a poodle. I would as leif hold discourse with a popinjay, as seek to draw out his wits; and I doubt what he has, are not often at home. He is so absent and thoughtful; and yet there is not that gentleness in his pensive humour, especially to us ladies, that should come of one that knows his love would be acceptable. What his clerkship may be to your Majesty's comfort, I know not; but truly he is like one of the supporters of your Majesty's arms, the unicorn: it hath but one horn, and he but one faculty, his music! It is a poor thing for so goodly a person to be able only to sing."

" Go to, Livingstone," said the Queen; " thou art letting thy tongue run away with thy discretion, he may have other cares than thou hast guessed at. We prove in ourself that there may be vexations enow in Scotland, without the anxieties of love."

By this time they had come almost close up to Chatelard, who, absorbed in his own medita-

tions, was not aware of their approach till he turned to walk back. The Queen, at the moment, was not disposed to notice him further, and the etiquette observed among her ladies, while in her presence, deterred Mary Livingstone from addressing him with more than a silent smile of recognition; but before they could move away he was on his knees, and supplicated the Queen with great fervour to pardon the father of Adelaide.

"I thought it was so, Livingstone," said the Queen. "But rise, Chatelard, we are better disposed to accede to your request than such humble entreaty would seem to anticipate. It is thought convenient that his trial should proceed, and by the result, our mercy, if it be needed, shall be fully granted."

Emboldened by this assurance, he ventured to reply with renewed entreaty, beseeching her Majesty, if the matter were so determined, to allay the agitation of Adelaide by extending the indulgence at once.

What the Abbot of Kilwinning urged upon that point had not been lost on the Queen; on

the contrary, she saw in the formality of a trial, the result of which it was predetermined should not be carried into effect, only a solemn mockery of justice, and, in consequence, the supplication of Chatelard produced a commensurate impression.

"In truth, Livingstone," said her Majesty, turning towards that young lady, "there is something too fine in this policy of a trial as a preliminary to a pardon. I have thought much of it all night; and my thoughts incline, for that and for many other reasons, to order the pardon to go forth at once."

Chatelard on hearing this re-urged his suit with redoubled zeal, and Mary, a little tired with his importunity, in the weariness of her spirit, said—"It shall be so." And, as was customary on conceding a grace, she presented him her hand to kiss, and then suddenly moved on without speaking until she was some ten or twelve paces away, when she said—

"Livingstone, this must be ended. That young man regards me too much as a woman, and forgets the humility due to my station; let

him not be permitted to come to us in the evening, nor until I shall have had time to consider of him."

Mary Livingstone smiled, and said,

" If he is in love, I'll wager my best earrings, and they are those your Majesty gave me, that it is with one that may not be named."

" Thou art too pert," said the Queen, " I prithee sheathe that sharp tongue of thine. I like its glitter, but its edge is dangerous."

Chatelard, exulting at the ready compliance with his solicitation, immediately left the garden; for, although he conceived his success to be entirely the effect of the Queen's partiality, he yet imagined that she did not choose to evince it, and that her tacit reproof was not incurred by his presumption, but was only a sacrifice to decorum.

In leaving the garden he met Adelaide advancing to join her Majesty, and with great warmth of satisfaction, congratulated her on the merciful determination of the Queen. At this juncture the Prior of St. Andrews accidentally joined them; but he partook not of their plea-

sure, when informed of Chatelard's success. On the contrary he appeared much discomposed, and moved with rapid steps towards the parterre in which the Queen was walking. Suddenly, however, he checked his speed, and returned; whilst Adelaide, full of gratitude and rejoicing, hastened to join the Queen. He had not, however, come many paces back, when he was met by the Earl of Morton, who had just parted from Rizzio.

" He is a deevilish clever hempy, that Dauvit Ritchie, or Rizzio, as we must name him amang the foreigners. The fellow has the e'e of a hawk, and a tongue that would wile the bird frae the tree. I'm thinking if we kent a thought more about him, and he would cast off his papistry, we might make something of him."

" If," replied the Protestant Prior, " you make it his interest, his papistry would soon be doffed. It's a loose cloak and sits easy on him."

" Say ye sae, James. Aye, ye're gayen auld farrent yourself; for I think wi' you that Dauvit's no very strait-laced. I would make his

plack a bawbee, to hae his servitude wi' his gude-will. He would make a capital tool in any bit plottie that the need of the times may oblige us to get up for the gude of the realm."

"Take care," replied the Prior, "that, in making him your tool, you don't find that he makes himself your master."

"Eh! James, but for an honest lad ye hae ill thoughts of other folk. I tell you that Dauvit is a very kind-hearted tod in his way, and I'm sure would do meikle for gratitude. The Queen has not amang a' her red-legged aliens a leiler servant."

"I hope he will prove so, my Lord," replied the Prior; "but I have got grievous tidings just now. Come with me, and I will tell you," and with this they quitted the garden together.

CHAPTER XVI.

" What is station high?
'Tis a proud mendicant; it boasts and begs:
It begs an alms of homage from the throng,
And oft the throng denies its charity."

OTHELLO.

THE determination of the Queen to pardon Knockwhinnie was soon generally known, and excited very little attention; for it had been expected by many as almost a necessary consequence of Adelaide being her favourite attendant. Southennan, before the news had reached him, went early to the Palace, where he found the Count Dufroy alone in the gallery, and in evident agitation, not on account of the pardon, but the manner in which it had been granted on the solicitation of Chatelard.

" I shall not long remain in Scotland," said

the Count; " Adelaide will soon be under the protection of her father, and my advice is no longer likely to be useful to the Queen. Nor were it as acceptable as I once flattered myself it was, your Scottish nobles are too apt to resent the interference of a foreigner in their national concerns, to make the condition of his service honourable. He must submit to suffer and endure, which does not well accord with the humour of my temper."

Southennan, with unaffected regret, lamented the decision of the Count. Having acquired some knowledge, both of France and England, he was sensible of defects in the manners of his countrymen, and was of the number of those who considered the intercourse with the former, which had been rendered so free while her Majesty resided there, as a public benefit. The arrival, with the Queen, of so many accomplished adherents and members of her French Court, he also regarded as calculated to continue that desirable intimacy.

" Perhaps," said Dufroy, " had I still enjoyed the confidence of the Queen, the rough-

ness of the nobles might not have so soon hastened my determination: but that being no longer allowed, my occupation is gone. To her, as the widow of France, my homage and service were due, and they were loyally performed; but I have no right nor claim to meddle in your troubled politics, nor motive to remain where I can only expect mortifications."

Southennan, not being yet aware that the pardon of Knockwhinnie had been granted upon the solicitation of Chatelard, or, at least, was so believed, expressed some degree of surprise at hearing the Count thus open in his dissatisfaction, and said—

"It gives me pain to think worth like yours should be so little esteemed here, that the apprehension of neglect moves you to leave us."

"Not the apprehension only, but the experience. Know you not that the Queen has pardoned Knockwhinnie?"

"I have heard it rumoured that she was likely to do so," replied our hero; "but I did not fear it would have been felt by you so much

as an injury, though acquainted with your sentiments respecting the nature of his offence."

"Then you cannot have heard in what manner it has been granted?"

"I have been but just told that it was expected: nor has it surprised me; so much has her Majesty been urged to it: last night she almost conceded as much to the Abbot of Kilwinning."

"Had she done it then," replied the Count, "and on the solicitation of one so valued, I might have been at question with myself on the propriety of the grace; but to refuse so good and great a man—a dignitary both of the church and realm—and yield on the first asking to one scarce better than a menial! Oh, shame!"

"Was it to Chatelard?"

"Would it were in my power, Southennan," cried the Count, with irrepressible emotion, "to give you a rude answer, for imputing the possibility of such weakness to her who, till this fatal morning, hath ever been untarnished as the pearl that can receive no stain. Alas! tis even as you have said."

"It grieves me exceedingly," replied our hero, "to see how deeply this matter affects you. I am in part to blame, having been the first to entreat the mediation of Chatelard."

"Why did you that? What suggestion moved you to think his mediation might be of any efficacy?"

The Count, in asking these two simple questions, appeared alarmed, and suddenly thrown off his guard, which Southennan observing, became confused; for he could not well answer either, without explaining his suspicions of Chatelard's attachment to the Queen.

"Have you noticed aught particular in her conduct towards him?" resumed Dufroy eagerly, without waiting for an answer.

"Not in hers," replied Southennan.

"But in his towards her? Is it so?" exclaimed the high-minded Frenchman; and he added, in a tone of affecting compassion, "'Truly, it must be so. The destiny of her family hath overtaken her: but it mitigates the misfortune that he had not dared of his own presumption to be so bold."

While they were thus speaking Rizzio happened to pass across the gallery, and Dufroy beckoned him to draw near.

" Can you, Rizzio," said he, as the Italian approached, " tell us how this miracle came to pass?"

" What miracle! of what do you speak, my Lord?"

" How! have you not heard that the Queen, upon the intercession of Chatelard, has ordered a pardon to Knockwhinnie?"

" Impossible!" exclaimed Rizzio. " Presumptuous as he is, he durst not have ventured on so bold a suit."

" Had he not been sure of success," rejoined the Count, with a sigh.

Rizzio, however, remarked that he might have been incited by his declared admiration of Adelaide.

" Yes," interposed Southennan: " it must be as you say." And he recapitulated what had passed when he spoke with Chatelard on the subject.

But the Count gave little heed to what he said, which Rizzio observing, rejoined—

"Might it not have happened from the importunity with which her Majesty has been so beset? She may have granted the pardon from annoyance, being unable to resist further solicitation."

"It is well and loyally said," rejoined the Count, "but how came he to have been so bold as to interfere at all. It is, in its complexion, an adventure not reconcileable to common causes."

Rizzio, conscious of the subtle part he had himself played in the business, was visibly disturbed by this remark—so much so as to attract the attention of Southennan, who, in ignorance of the cause, said, respectfully—

"May it not be, my Lord, that this whole affair is too largely estimated? To you the rashness of Knockwhinnie must be a thing of serious recollection; but the world, which has no special interest to remember it, will set little account on the pardon."

The Count looked at him gravely, and then

added, with a steadily-sustained voice, approaching to severity,

"Think you it is the pardon that molests me; or that I can repine because the Queen has exercised the fairest attribute of royalty? No, Southennan; I am grieved only because she has conceded to Chatelard a favour refused to better men, and that too, in opposition to the wisdom of her Chancellor. It is a thing in itself, perhaps, of small importance; but, by the manner in which it has been done, it may be made serious. I pray to Heaven that evil may not come of it."

All this anxiety appeared to our hero disproportioned to the cause. He thought there was, perhaps, something of envy in the tone with which Dufroy expressed himself concerning Chatelard, especially as he was persuaded that some lurking resentment still affected his disposition towards Knockwhinnie. But the alteration in the countenance of Rizzio, when the Count remarked that the proceeding of Chatelard was not to be accounted for by ordinary causes, haunted his imagination; and he suspected the Italian of being in some way a party

to it. He, however, said nothing, deeming it prudent, in the dissatisfied mood of the Count, to refrain from any question or observation which might have the effect of exciting it still more. Dufroy himself was not inclined to continue the conversation.

The more the Count reflected on the transaction, he became the less content with his information. He discerned, by his innate perspicacity, that some peculiar instigation had influenced the conduct of Chatelard; and he was convinced it could not be the effect of that attachment only which he professed to cherish for Adelaide; for he was, in common with many of the Court doubtful of its sincerity. In fine, he could not but entertain a derogatory suspicion of the Queen; and he resolved, in consequence, out of the true and dignified loyalty with which he was actuated, to avail himself once more of the freedom she had allowed to him on all occasions, to point out the hazard she ran of incurring the forfeiture of those golden opinions which her people seemed then so willing to treasure up for her.

CHAPTER XVII.

" Officious fool! that must needs meddling be
In business that concerns not thee."
COWLEY.

SOUTHENNAN parted from Rizzio at the same time that the Count Dufroy retired. He was too well satisfied that Knockwhinnie had received a pardon, to feel any particular interest in the means by which it had been obtained. It seemed to him, however, that Rizzio had been in some way accessary to the application of Chatelard, although he evidently wished not to be known in the transaction. These reflections passed through his mind as he was retiring, and some degree of curiosity was in consequence excited. He was too ingenuous himself to suspect others of sinister intentions, nor could he

account for the embarrassment which the Italian appeared to suffer, as if an act of benevolence had been one of shame.

As he went out at the portal of the Palace he met Chatelard in a state of flushed exultation; his countenance was elated, and a vibratory emotion visibly affected his whole frame; his eyes were eager and unsteady, insomuch that he neither could look another firmly in the face, nor bear the inquisition of any eye bent upon his own. There was moreover an increased style of courtesy, bland and patronizing, in his manners, and an altogetherness of grace and condescension in his air and deportment which, to our hero, seemed incomprehensibly disproportioned to his circumstances. Their reciprocal salutations were stiff in their mode; with more, however, of an apparently assumed restraint on both sides, than of any actual diminution of intimacy.

Southennan congratulated him on the success of his application to the Queen, and cordially thanked him from himself for the favour he had been the means of procuring for his friend

Knockwhinnie, adding, however, in a tone tinged as it were with irony.

"This cannot fail to secure your triumph with Adelaide. It must have been to you delightful to tell her how you had succeeded."

"I have scarcely seen her since," replied Chatelard.

"Was it not in her name you applied to her Majesty?"

Chatelard seemed a little confused at this question, but evidently gratified; for he answered in a simpering, half earnest, half jocular voice, that it was almost by an accident he had succeeded; and he then described how he had met the Queen and Lady Mary Livingstone in the garden.

"But how came you to think of applying at all, every other application having failed?"

"Of my own modesty," replied the Frenchman with a laugh, at the same time blushing, "I should not have undertaken the adventure; but Rizzio encouraged me."

"Indeed! to help your suit with Adelaide!" said Southennan. "But I must carry the glad

news to her father," and with these words he wished Chatelard good morning.

He was not surprised to hear that Rizzio, who had so recently affected to know nothing of the pardon, had really been at the bottom of the whole affair: and he could only account for his equivocation, by supposing that he was afraid lest his interference might be resented by the Count Dufroy. It seemed a strange business: and yet there was nothing in the incidents of it which ought to have surprised him, farther than that Chatelard should have dared to approach the Queen after so great a dignitary as the Abbot of Kilwinning had been obliged to retire unsatisfied.

These thoughts passed rapidly through his mind, as he slowly ascended the Canongate. In the midst of them a hand was familiarly laid on his shoulder, and, on turning round, he found Rizzio at his side in a state of inward enjoyment, with that expression in his countenance of crafty gratification which is always the consequent and disagreeable index of triumphant cunning. Our hero on seeing him also

smiled, and inquired, why it was that he had pretended to Dufroy ignorance of Chatelard's proceeding, when in fact he was the father of it.

Rizzio was, as the sailors say, taken aback by this sudden question, not being aware that Southennan had met with Chatelard; but he was ever too much the master of himself to be long disconcerted, and accordingly with his wonted readiness he replied,

"In sooth, Southennan, it seems but a thankless service to do you any good. You know that Chatelard's passion for Adelaide is but mere painting—a semblance without substance—a glow without fire or flame; while yours is all fire, and yet shows no gleam which she regards. Now what if I thought it would help your cause, to show her to what aim his wishes were bent? Might it not have the effect to turn her eyes in some measure from him to you, by making the Queen's true sentiments visible?"

This was said in so artificial a manner, that Southennan was convinced of its insincerity, and

felt as if there were something in the very nature of Rizzio to be distrusted: he made no answer further than by remarking, in a jocular manner, at the same time looking impressively at the Italian,

" You are too shrewd: such management as love seems to require at Court, would frighten simple country folks to fly from it. It is enough to make the snared bird struggle until it has snapped the springe."

Rizzio, however, had by this time fully recovered his self-possession, and contrived, as they walked up the street together, plausibly almost to persuade Southennan that he had been animated, in the incitement of Chatelard, entirely by a wish to serve him.

" In truth, my friend," said he, " let us look at this affair reasonably, as we should do. The fellow has talked so much of his wounded heart, and ardent passion for Adelaide, that no one believes a word he says about it; and you and I have not been unobservant spectators of who is the true loadstone of his affections; and, therefore, so that her Majesty be not offended, all

stratagems are fair to get him out of your way."

By this time they had come near the entrance to the Unicorn, at the door of which Balwham was accidentally looking out. Rizzio, being bound to the house, walked at once in, and Southennan would have proceeded up the street, but Balwham came hastily to him, and said,

"A word wi' you, Southennan!" who accordingly turned, and went with him into his private room.

"Oh dear," cried Balwham, as soon as they were in and the door shut; "Isna' this a dreadfu' concern; a' the town's in a hobbleshaw; the Provost is louping about the Council-room like a frightened water-wag-tail in a cage, and the Bailies and a' the Counsellors are sitting in a consternation, like puddocks on the lip o' a well."

Our hero's thoughts running on Knockwhinnie's pardon, attributed this alarming state of the magistracy to something unpopular which had resulted from it; whereas, the worthy host was speaking of the amazement which the dis-

covery of Auchenbrae's escape, and the substitution of Cornylees had occasioned. Under this misconception, Southennan replied,

"I hope the agitation will soon subside, and that the people will incline to the side of mercy."

"I would fain houp sae too; but I am just terrified out o' my seven senses, for they say that the instigators, and a' that were art and part in it, are to be brought to condign punishment."

"Oh! you don't say so. Is it already come to that?"

"Na, for any thing I ken to the contrary, Thomas Noose, the hangman, may hae gotten his commands; for Johnnie Gaff is dismissed. Puir creature! he was here telling me o' the interlocutor, and was in sic a panic that he would hae dwamed had I no gi'en him a tass o' Lode-vic."

"You astonish me."

"'Deed, I 'm astonished mysel', for he counselled me to tak leg bail."

You!" exclaimed Southennan, "what had you to do with it?"

"Me! I'm an honest man, Southennan, a lang-respected member o' the Vintners' Company: what I did was for the best, and scaith was as far frae my thoughts as frae the bairn's that's unborn."

"But, in the name of all that is wonderful, how came you to be, in any way whatever, connected with Monsieur Chatelard?"

"Eh! preserve me, is he in the frying-pan too? What's his transgression, and how cam' he to be conjunc' wi' us?"

"With us—with you," cried Southennan; what is it that you say?"

"Hae ye no heard that the Tolbooth had been broken, and Auchenbrae aff and awa', leaving Cornylees, your ain friend, for a nest-egg to cleck mischief out o'? I thought the whole town kent this, and I was just keeking out at the door to see if there was a crowd coming to tak me up, for flee the country I winna'. I hae a conscience void o' offence, baith to man and beast. And what would come o' the Unicorn and a'

the gentleman? It's fash enough wi' a' my forethought, to get their dinner as it is!"

Southennan perceived that they had been at cross purposes, but without explaining the source of his own misconception, he inquired into the particulars of Balwham's story, and immediately after quickened his steps towards the Tolbooth.

CHAPTER XVIII.

"I am undone; there is no living, none,
If Bertram be away!"
SHAKSPEARE.

IN the meantime the Count Dufroy had requested an audience of the Queen; which her Majesty, unconscious of having done any thing equivocal, was surprised at. It had been the custom of the Count, at all hours after she had come for the day into the presence-chamber, to obtain admission without the formality of asking leave. She was still more surprised when on his entrance she saw by his countenance that something had occurred to disturb him; and there was a thoughtful sadness in his eye which made her feel as if she had given occasion for some remonstrance or exhortation. In consequence, she stood waiting until he should address her.

A reception so reserved and so unusual was attributed by him to the consciousness of error; and he spoke to her with an unwonted degree of solemnity:

"Madam, I have just been informed that your Majesty has been pleased to extend your royal mercy to Knockwhinnie."

The Queen with a pensive smile replied that it was so.

"But," said she, "I cannot hope that your stern justice will applaud the deed!"

"It is not to the clemency by which your Majesty's benevolence has been gratified, that I would presume to object; but I would be assured that it has not been granted in the manner I have been informed."

The Queen smiled, and said, with her usual affability, "And what is the contingency if it has been so?"

The Count paused to meditate his answer, and then said, with the profoundest respect, "I shall return to France."

The Queen looked in the utmost amazement, and then said, struggling with emotion,

"Can I have done anything to cause me to forfeit such estimable service? Count Dufroy, I have here few friends; there may be around me honest men, but I know not yet which to trust; and therefore, I beseech—I would almost say command, you—to stifle that intention, granting that I have erred. But in what consists my error?"

Dufroy paused again before he replied, and then said,

"In conceding to the young man Chatelard the pardon of Knockwhinnie, in opposition to higher and graver advice; and after your Majesty had deemed it expedient to refuse the application of the Abbot of Kilwinning."

A blush overspread the Queen's countenance. She discerned at once his whole mind, and saw the construction of which her compliance was susceptible; but she added firmly,

"How know you that the pardon was granted at the request of Chatelard?"

"It is so stated: if it be not true, none of all your Majesty's faithfulest subjects will more rejoice than myself."

"Is there, then," exclaimed the Queen in evident alarm, "so much importance fastened to my consenting that the pardon should go forth, merely because Chatelard was made the agent of my intention."

"It is to be deplored that your Majesty had not consented to the solicitation of the Abbot of Kilwinning, or to any other of your Court, rather than to that presumptuous young man."

"Heavens!" cried the Queen, with increasing alarm, and resuming her seat, "What do your words portend? What is said of me, that you, from that true loyalty which I have ever experienced, should deem it needful to speak so plainly? Tell me, what is it that you think? As for the babbling gossip of the Court, I account it but as the east wind."

"And that is blighting," replied the Count; and advancing towards her, he knelt, and she extended to him her hand to kiss. "Pardon my boldness! In these times and in this country I fear your Majesty may not lightly consider the mildew of such detraction; there are many of high power and great influence in the king-

dom, who look upon your Majesty's religion as an obstacle to the ascendancy they covet in the State. I grieve, more than words can express, that Chatelard is so honoured by your Majesty."

The Queen started up, her eyes flashing with indignation, and, after hastily moving across the room, said,

"My Lord—no, let me rather say my friend—speak with your wonted candour! I will not disguise that I am now well aware of all you think; but on what show of evidence or of conjecture dare any one suspect, that in this grace I was infected with any unbecoming motive?"

It was impossible for the Count not to feel the sincerity of this impassioned address; and he immediately replied, with his old accustomed freedom, that of her Majesty nothing derogatory had ever been insinuated till this unfortunate occurrence; and he added more sedately, that the ill-placed attachment of Chatelard was evident to the whole Court.

"Has it, indeed, been so observed?"

"Then," said the Count, drily, "your Majesty knows it, and yet encouraged his presump-

tion, by granting to him a request denied to others?"

"Encouraged! Can the Count Dufroy say so?" And she burst into a passion of tears, exclaiming, "Yes, I have done wrong; but it was not from any estimation of him: my spirit was worn out by the importunities I have endured: his application was but the atom that turned the scale. Do with him, Count, as you deem most accordant with my honour; let him be instantly sent forth the kingdom."

The Count stood for some time viewing her with compassion, as she walked across the room, abandoned to grief, and indulging her tears. In the midst of this agitation, she suddenly halted, and, turning towards him, said,

"I see, in doing that, we shall only give warranty to the venom of slanderous tongues; and yet what else can be done?"

Dufroy attempted to console her, by assuring her of his conviction, that as there had been no oblivion of her own dignity, the story might pass away, when Chatelard should be sent home to France.

"But," said the Queen, "how can he remain here without some change being shown to him in my demeanour. Will not that be observed? and how can I stoop to dissimulation with his audacity? No, Count, there is no other course; send him forth the kingdom!"

"I fear there is none other," added the Count. "I did think a middle course might have been steered; but your Majesty's condition forbids all expediency."

"Then let him be at once informed his service is dispensed with, and that he come no more to this house. I can make sacrifices of things dear to me when need requires; but this is none. I did not suspect that his measureless arrogance had been so noted by others!"

Adelaide entering at this moment, the Count retired, and the Queen, bending upon her shoulder, again wept bitterly.

"Alas, Madam, is he still so ruthless?" said Adelaide; "while all the Court rejoice in your Majesty's clemency?"

The Queen, instead of replying to this appeal, abruptly inquired,

"Have you observed in Chatelard aught towards me to justify the malice of evil tongues. Answer me plainly, for you can have been no negligent observer of him. You do not answer. It is enough, and I forgive you. But tell me sincerely, have ever I, by accident or inadvertency, showed him any particular favour?"

"I have not myself," replied Adelaide, with diffidence and gentleness; "but I have been told, that on more than one occasion your Majesty has been too gracious to him."

"Who dare say so?" cried the indignant Queen. "It is some idle fancy of the antechamber. Twice he touched my hand with too much of fellowship; and I made him conscious he was too bold. But such foolery cannot be again: he is dismissed my service; and by the first vessel and favouring wind he goes to France."

This sudden intelligence smote the enthralled heart of Adelaide; she became pale, and, almost swooning, sank into a seat.

"Why, thou weak girl, what hath overcome thee? Verily, thou art more forward in thy love

than accords with modesty. I take blame upon myself for not reproving thy too-well-seen affection before. He is not worthy of it; nor doth it much enhance thy discretion, to have made such a choice, when one so far surpassing him in all manly and mannerly excellence is pining unrequited. Think no more of him; and give such heed to young Southennan as in time may draw that cherished folly from thy breast. But I will urge thee no further at this time, than that thou shouldst prepare to meet thy father with happy looks; for doubtless he will presently be in quest of thee here. Go then, and set thy countenance in better plight. It would argue little for thy good-nature, which has hitherto been all gentleness, to meet thy father with a visage so woe-begone. Go at once, and send in Livingstone. Verily, she is a better companion for one who hath discarded a suitor, than the hapless nymph who long in hopelessness hath loved too well!"

CHAPTER XIX.

―――― " With what greediness
Do I hug my afflictions ! there is no mirth
Which is not truly season'd with some madness."
FORD.

KNOCKWHINNIE, from the time of his incarceration, had suffered much in his mind. He did not greatly dread the ignominy, nor the result of his trial, being persuaded that as his offence had not proved fatal, the indictment would be restricted to an arbitrary punishment, according to a prerogative which the public prosecutor of Scotland, the Lord Advocate, has long exercised; but still his anxieties were sharp and manifold.

He had been now for a long period of years absent from his lands and castle, which, in the interval, had fallen into decay. He thought the Lord Kilburnie, his father-in-law, had acted towards him with a rigour that could only be

justified by some great wrong, and he was unconscious of having committed any towards him. He considered him as the spring of all his domestic misfortunes, by having, as he supposed, influenced the Lady Ellenor to remain in Scotland when she was so earnestly entreated to come to France. His heart was also troubled on his daughter's account, both with respect to the state of her affections, and the relationship in which she stood to the Count Dufroy by the adoption; for habitual reflection, even after he had ascertained the innocence of that high-minded nobleman, made him still think of him with something of the heat and irritation of an enemy. But the chiefest source of his annoyance arose from the confinement.

Accustomed to the freedom, activity, and adventure of an outlaw, he felt as if his spirit were girded within a hoop, and he moved in agitation through his gloomy chamber, like a wild bird when first imprisoned. This physical suffering, however, for it was of that nature, though arising from the ineffectual struggles of his mind, subsided in the course of the first night, and by the

time Southennan was admitted to him, a gloomy melancholy had succeeded to the vivid emotions and sudden fluctuation with which he was at first so violently affected. In its calm, however, there was no peace. It was like the unwholesome fen, which in its sullen silence breathes forth infection. He became afflicted with misanthropical antipathies; his reminiscences were sour and indigestible; and his spirit, sickened with the nausea of self-dissatisfaction, revolted against the world for the sufferings he endured, unjustly disproportioned, as he thought them, to the extent of his errors.

When Southennan entered he was standing near the grated aperture of his dungeon, into which a dim reflection of the sun from the glass of an opposite window, shone with a dull and sallow lustre upon the ruins of his tall and manly form; his arms were folded on his breast, and his head was slightly bent in rumination.

On hearing the door opened he turned round his eyes without changing his position, and on observing that it was not the jailor who entered,

he assumed a proud attitude until his visitor had come into the light.

Our hero advanced with cheerfulness; and, animated with the news he had to tell, held out to him both his hands. Knockwhinnie coldly acknowledged the warmth of his friendly eagerness, and with a seeming reluctance touched only one of them.

Southennan, though sensible of this ungracious return, suppressed his feelings, and joyously told him that the Queen had consented to his immediate pardon, and that he might expect his release in the course of the day.

At this important information the mood and temper of the prisoner underwent no immediate change. He heard it with apparent indifference, and only enquired for his daughter.

"How is this Knockwhinnie?" said Southennan; "you hear me as if I were the bearer of some household errand."

"'Tis even so, and I am grieved at being unable to return your zeal and ardour with but the words of thankfulness. This dark, damp, narrow chamber, and the prohibited door,

have chilled my heart with a morose torpidity. I am a thing discharged of its uses—of a humour to be pleased with a sight of miseries."

Southennan remonstrated with him on the indulgence of such unprofitable fancies, and endeavoured to dispel his dejection; but until the officer with the pardon had been admitted, all argument was unavailing. His countenance, however, then brightened, and when he reached the open street, he fetched a long deep breath, as if he drank a refreshing draught, and said,

"How delicious is the free air—how wide the path of liberty!"

They had proceeded together to Knockwhinnie's lodgings, where he dressed himself for the Palace, being eager to visit his daughter, before Southennan recollected what the host of the Unicorn had told him of Cornylees' confinement. This induced them to separate; for our hero was constrained by his humanity to hasten back to the Tolbooth.

Knockwhinnie had not proceeded many steps down the street, when suddenly recollecting that

he had neglected to inquire to whose mediation he was indebted for his pardon, he hastily turned back, and overtaking our hero, begged to be informed as to this.

The question was discordant to Southennan's feelings. It implied a sense of obligation on the part of Knockwhinnie: but he, however, disdained to conceal that his gratitude was due to Chatelard.

"Say you it was the young Frenchman!" exclaimed Knockwhinnie, "he who professes such affection for my daughter?"

Our hero felt, as it were, the chill shadow of a cloud overcome his spirit, and he replied in a marked and emphatic manner,

"The same. He does indeed openly profess the most inextinguishable love—too openly."

He would have added more, but was restrained by motives of delicacy. He knew that the gossip of the Court would soon set the professions of Chatelard in their proper light; and he therefore rejected the suggestion as mean, which prompted himself, though but for an instant, to think of deteriorating the grateful

sensibility by which Knockwhinnie was then animated. But his fears were awakened; for by this time he had learnt enough of Court practices to think it not beyond the scope of probability, that Chatelard would accept the hand of Adelaide, to disguise the daring and ambitious passion which he had cherished for the Queen, and which he so sedulously but insufficiently endeavoured to conceal.

CHAPTER XX.

―――― " We are prepared,
And easily entreated; 'tis good manners
Not to be troublesome!"
FORD.

SOUTHENNAN did not find it necessary to proceed so far as the Tolbooth, for he met Cornylees coming from the Council-chamber, where he had been before the magistrates, by whom, after his case had been examined, he was discharged.

"In course now, Southennan," said the exasperated Laird, "this is an awful business; but it's weel o'er, and I must thole the dule o't as weel as I can. Oh, Laird! it's a most horridable thing, in course now, to be kept in the black-hole o' a Tolbooth, frae the yesterday till the morn."

Southennan expressed great pleasure at see-

ing the Laird again at liberty; and it being now nearly dinner time, he returned with him towards the Unicorn.

"I think, Cornylees," said he, "it was not becoming your wonted sagacity to be taken in by Auchenbrae?"

"Ye may weel say, taken in; for I had nae business, in course now, wi' him. How I was put into his hole, and how he got out, is past the comprehensions of human nature. It might, in a sense, hae come of Balwham's auld sherries. Hech! but it's stout and gude. I wouldna' mind to hae a crack wi' you, anent my disasters, in course now, o'er a flask o't."

In this sort of clishmaclavering they approached the door of the tavern, at which Hughoc was waiting for his master.

For some reason or another the boy, on this occasion, did not seem in any particular manner to wish for a private interview; but before Southennan appeared in sight, he had been remarkably sharp on the outlook for him, running continually into the street, and holding his hand over his eyes to see if he were coming, either

from his own lodgings in the upper part of the town, or from Holyrood House below; indeed, his anxiety and impatience were so remarkable, that his conduct attracted the notice of some of the other guests.

As his master passed into the door, Hughoc slyly pulled him by the skirt, and with a significant cautious look, intimated that he had something particular to communicate: our hero, in consequence, allowed Cornylees to go up stairs alone, and lingered in the passage to hear what the boy had to say. Hughoc, however, thought the place too public; he looked suspiciously around, and then said—

"Come into Maister Balwham's ain room, and I'll brush the stour aff you, Laird!"

All this mystery had the intended effect on Southennan: he followed Hughoc into the room, and closed the door behind him, saying—

"Well, what have you got to tell me now; be quick, for dinner will soon be on the table."

"Ye maun first," replied the boy, "say, as sure's death, that ye'll no speak o't! for the man that told me said it was a something that

might bring life and limb into jeopardy." And he added, with a soft and low solemn whisper, " They say it's a treason!"

" Let me hear what it is."

" The Queen's in a terrible passion; running up and down the palace, whisking in at ae door, and vanishing out at anither, like a cat wi' a gale o' wind in her tail."

" And for what is all this?"

" A French gentleman has daur't to court her, which is a sin, they say, that canna' be pardoned, and which I am weel pleased to hear; for when I saw her royal Majesty gallanting wi' her leddies, I thought she was just like anither lass, though a very bonnie ane."

Southennan was amused at this description, and inquired what he imagined the Queen to have been.

" Na," said Hughoc; " that's a kittle question. But I thought she was a' gold and pearls, wi' a crown on her head, and bairns holding up her tail. Gudeness me! what's the worth o' kings and queens, if the're only just like other folk?"

" Well, but what is this story of the Frenchman ? "

" The rights o't cows a': he fell down, as the clash gangs, on his bended knees, and began to say a pater-noster, when the Count came in and catched him, and hauled him out o' the room by the lug and the horn, and flung him down the stair, wi' a kick that made him tumble the wull-cat three times before he reached the bottom."

" And what then ? "

" He's ordered to pack up his ends and his awls, and be awa' to France."

Notwithstanding the extravagance of this story, Southennan discovered something in it which he was not ill-pleased to hear. It was manifest that Chatelard had committed some indiscretion, and that the Count Dufroy had dismissed him from the Queen's service. In fact, the boy's tale was but the vulgar version of the circumstances which have been already related, with the addition, however, of Chatelard's dismissal. Hughoc was enjoined to observe secresy; and our hero went up stairs

into the room where the daily guests were assembling. Here the particulars of different editions of the same story were under the process of collation and dissection; but all agreed that Chatelard had been dismissed, and that sentence of banishment was issued against him.

Cornylees, who had listened attentively to the discussion, and still resentful of the incarceration he had suffered, placed himself at table beside our hero, with a troubled and gloomy countenance. During the whole operations of the dinner he continued moody and sullen; at last he said—

"When will ye be gaun west, in course now, Southennan? I'll be aff the morn; an honest man has nae security in Embro. There was I, for naething waur than a drap of drink, confined, the best part of twa days and a whole blessed night, in the dismallest room, and the cauldest, in course now, I believe in this world! Jonah, in the whale's belly, without fire or candle, and naething a' the time but cauld fish guts to handle, wasna waur aff. And here's a young man, who just, I 'se warrant, for calling the

Queen, in course now, a bonnie birdie, has lost his bread. I'm thinking courts and capitals are no canny places, and my back shall be, in course now, soon fronting them baith. But, Southennan, as ye're thinking I see of staying a while, in course now, ye'll be needing new claes, and ye ken the suit I got for the Reception was of the best o' Genoesy. I'll let you hae a bargain of them; and in the hope that we may make it gude, what say ye to a flask of Balwham's auld sherries?"

A flask was accordingly ordered, but our hero declined the Laird's court dress, and advised him to carry it with him to the west country, where it might be shown as an honesty, to the latest posterity.

"Weel, I dinna think that advice, Southennan, ill waur't on me, in course now; for I had a thought o' the same sort mysel: but in the way o' a politic frugality, I thought that if I kept the breeks for a memento mori, or as I may say, a memento Mary, cause they were torn in course now, when I fell by my misfortune in the Royal presence, that it would be sufficient." And giving Southennan a knudge with his el-

bow, and chuckling as he did so, he added, "Many a gude laugh will my posteriors hae, when they see the rents as testimonials of my exploits at the bonnie widow's court!"

At this juncture, Balwham wiping the flask with his apron, placed it open on the table.

"There," said he, "with triumph, "is a better cordial than any in a' the Queen's aught. I had it out o' the cellar, ready for my worthy friend, Knockwhinnie. Ave Maria! he's now a free man; and I had a hope he would hae honoured my table by taking a trencher here, as he was wont to do in the Queen mother's time. But, hech sirs! he's an altered and penitential man! Oh, Cornylees! little ken ye o' what I 'm subjected to on account o' your spree in his behalf. It was weel intended, but the best o' folk, as weel as you Laird, are liable to mak' a mistake at a time."

Southennan, who stood, as Cornylees said of him, " more on his peremptors than was comely in the stock of an ancient house, or becoming the gude auld fashions o' Scotland," did not entirely relish the freedom of his host; and accor-

dingly he civilly gave him a hint to retire.—" Well, Southennan, that beats prent, to tell an honest man in his ain house that we couldna' be fashed wi' him! In course now, I wouldna' hae been guilty o' sic menseless breeding for the price of my velvet dress, the whilk ye havena', in course now, yet said ye would buy."

Much as, at all times, our hero was amused with the homespun eccentricities of Cornylees, the story of Hughoc had left an impression which he could not shake off; and in consequence he had but taken two glasses of the wine, when, on pretence of business, he left the Laird to solace his solitude with the remainder.

CHAPTER XXI.

> "——— This is some fellow
> Who, having been prais'd for bluntness, doth affect
> A saucy roughness; and constrains the garb
> Quite from his nature."
>
> SHAKSPEARE.

THE reader has already been informed that the Earl of Morton was, at this period, a distinguished member of the Scottish Court. This nobleman acted an eminent part in the subsequent troubles of Mary's reign, and was raised in the end to the dignity of Regent of the Kingdom.

He was esteemed by all parties as a man of talent: he professed to be a Protestant, and had great influence with that party; but his conduct was loose and licentious, compared to the strict morality of the other lords of the congregation;

and it was not imputed to him that any principle, either of religion or of probity, stood in the way of his interest or advancement.

In his manners, Morton was coarse and familiar; and possessed a downright blunt humour, which persons of that sort of character often assume and practice, as an evidence of what is called plain honesty, but which would better deserve the name of rough roguery. His person was not unlike his mind: he was rather under the common size; his limbs and figure indicated weight rather than strength; he was massy rather than athletic, dark in his complexion, his head round and bald; and his features, harsh and without harmony, were expressive of shrewdness, fearlessness, and more of irascible obstinacy than of fortitude. Being addicted to court popularity among the lower orders, his language was in consequence colloquial, often vulgar: but his humour served to redeem the vulgarity, and the strong grasp of seeming sense which he took in his remarks, sometimes procured more deference to his opinions, than the degree of their wisdom deserved: in his wisdom, indeed, there was

much of cunning; and he was better pleased to accomplish his purposes by craftiness, than by that plain straightforward course, which he so much affected.

When Knockwhinnie, after changing his dress, proceeded to Holyrood House, to see his daughter, he fell in with the Earl of Morton, with whom he had been, in his youth, acquainted. Time had, however, so altered himself in the interval, that the Earl did not recognise him at first, when he addressed himself to him, so that Knockwhinnie was obliged to mention his name, and to remind him of their former companionship.

"Aye!" said his Lordship, with one of his gruff smiles, "and so ye're that outlawed ne'er-do-well: but I hear ye hae gotten your pardon. I wonder what ye'll make o't, for when I was acquaint wi' you lang syne, ye were as camstairie a swankie as any royster in Lithgow or Falkland, and I maun say ye're no blate to be shoving your snout so soon in amang us here. What's your business at the Palace?"

Knockwhinnie recollected enough of Mor-

ton's character to take this address as it was really meant, and with equal jocularity answered it, saying,

"My daughter is there with the Queen, and I have not seen her since she was an infant."

"A brave father ye hae been to her!" said Morton; "and what's her name, and what's she like?"

Knockwhinnie briefly recapitulated the circumstances of her adoption by the Count Dufroy, to which Morton listened with curiosity and attention, without interposing a word during the recital, but at the conclusion he said,

"And so that jimp and genty lily-faced lassie, the Queen's mamselle, as they call her, is your only daughter. She'll be weel tochered; but I doubt the straemash that has happened this morning will be a bar to her matrimony."

"To what do you allude?"

"Hae ye no heard that the Frenchman wi' the parrot's neb, that every body said was to marry the Count's daughter, is thought to hae been o'er girt wi' the Queen, and used his efficacy to get your pardon for glaumor to hide their gallanting."

Knockwhinnie was disturbed by this information. It augured, he considered, but ill for himself that Chatelard should have incurred the envy and malice of the courtiers for procuring his pardon, nor was he less troubled to hear such a cause assigned for his success, as that which the Earl so irreverently expressed.

By this time they had come near to the palace-gate, and were about to enter, when Morton seeing Chatelard and Rizzio at a distance, seemingly in earnest and serious conversation, pointed him out to Knockwhinnie.

" D'ye see," said he, " yon twa lads at the park-yett; ane of them is a perfect deevil incarnate. I mean him wi' the bowly legs, sae stout and short. I redd you, Knockwhinnie, take care of your lugs and the eyne in your head, to say naething of either your teeth or your tongue, for he has the black art of getting the better of every body. The other lad wi' the lang genteel legs, and sae spruce, is the Frenchman that got you respited frae the gallows; for its but a respite, Knockwhinnie, as nae doubt ye ken in your own breast what ye 're ordained for."

Knockwhinnie rather abruptly quitted the Earl, and went towards Rizzio and Chatelard. On approaching them, he addressed himself at once to the Frenchman, with his best courtesy, and thanked him with sincerity for the service he had done him; saying,

" I am Knockwhinnie, and I hope it is not true that you have been exposed to any ill-will on my account."

While he was speaking, Rizzio observed him closely, perusing him as it were from head to foot, an instinctive habit whenever a stranger came before him. Chatelard, on the contrary, appeared confused, his eye wandered, and every thing about him evinced a wish that he were elsewhere. The warmth, however, and frankness of Knockwhinnie, put this out of his power; they were too sincere and decided to be evaded, he could not, therefore, but acknowledge that he was happy in having been able to render any service to the father of Adelaide.

" It is true," said he, " that I have fallen since into some eclipse, but I accuse only Dufroy."

"What say you?" cried Knockwhinnie. "In what has he injured you? Is it on my account? Has he not already punished me enough?"

Rizzio, by a slight emotion of surprise, showed that he felt some interest in the father of Adelaide, whom he now saw for the first time. But he made no remark: Chatelard, however, replied,

"The Count is jealous of every one that has any influence with the Queen; and it is known that he was averse to your pardon. I succeeded in my application to her Majesty; and in that I have offended. He thinks, by having procured my dismissal, he has indemnified himself, and punished me: but I am not yet out of Scotland."

There was, in these few words, more of the spirit of a young man than the worldliness of a courtier. They implied confidence in the Queen's supposed partiality for him, more openly than was discreet towards a stranger. Rizzio seemed to feel this, and by a sign intimated to Chatelard to be more on his guard; but the pride and ambition of the Frenchman were both

smarting with the pain of his dismissal; at the time he was little disposed to repress the animosity which he felt against Dufroy, and accordingly he continued to inveigh against him, with the acrimony of mortified feelings and disappointed ambition.

"His enmity," said Knockwhinnie, "can only serve to augment my obligations to you; it indeed increases your claim upon me: and as he adopted my daughter without my consent, I am now, thanks to you and the Queen's grace, in a condition to assert the rights and prerogatives of her natural parent."

Rizzio, who had not before interposed, observed,

"But Chatelard is compelled to quit the kingdom, and is ordered to embark to-morrow in a vessel which sails in the course of the day for Calais."

"It must not be—it must not be!" rejoined Knockwhinnie, hastily; "he has obtained the remission of my offence, and it is my duty to mitigate his misfortune. In what odour stands Lord Morton with the Queen? he was once a

friend of mine, and I parted from him just now seemingly content to renew our intimacy. Think you that it will serve my friend here to ask his interference?"

"You are, no doubt, aware," replied Rizzio, "that he is with the reformers; but he hath power through the Queen's bastard brother, the Prior of St. Andrew's, and no man of the Court, not even the Count Dufroy, has, at this time, so much influence with her Majesty."

"Has the Prior too fallen from the church?" inquired Knockwhinnie, who was himself a Catholic, but a very moderate one.

"That is an old story," said Rizzio, "and it is supposed he will soon cast his slough: he is expected to be ennobled."

A slight shade of sadness passed over the countenance of Knockwhinnie, and he said, in a softened tone,

"I expect to find many old friends with new faces."

"If you find any friends at all," said Chatelard, "account yourself fortunate; for the Count Dufroy rules all."

"I grieve to hear it; our Scottish barons are not of a temper to brook the interference of foreigners in their concerns."

Rizzio changed colour at this, and said, "The man must be careless of his hands, who would attempt to use any freedom with your thistles."

"And yet," replied Chatelard, somewhat jeeringly, "I know of no one so apt as yourself to do so."

"What?" cried Rizzio, with a sharp accent.

"I have heard," replied the Frenchman, "that you are to be my successor."

Rizzio, whose situation in the office of the Queen's correspondence, was under Chatelard, affected to laugh at this, and looked at Knockwhinnie, who replied,

"In sooth, gentlemen, you must set a watch on your lips, if you hope for easy days and sound rest among us; for we do not account the state to have much prospered since it became needful to trust so much of our business to you learned foreigners. But I shall have other op-

portunities of counselling you on this head; and I pray you," he added, addressing Chatelard, " to meet me in the evening in the Unicorn, for I have not at present time to speak more of my mind to you."

CHAPTER XXII.

*" Lips busy and eyes fix'd, foot falling slow,
Arms hanging idly down, hands clasp'd below
Interpret to the marking eye distress,
Such as its symptoms can alone express."*
COWPER.

WHEN Knockwhinnie parted from Rizzio and Chatelard they walked into the Park, one of the most lonesome places in all the world so near to a royal residence and a great city. It lies between the Palace and Arthur's Seat, not exactly in a valley, but in a shallow hollow between the mountain and the rising ground that spreads up towards the Calton Hill. In those days a high wall inclosed the garden of Holyrood House on the one side, so that nothing could be seen from the bottom of the Park but St. Anthony's Chapel and the cliffs of the mountain, and the high, abrupt, and misty precipices of Salisbury Craigs.

The climate of this solitary retreat, if the expression may be allowed, was as bleak as the scene was dreary, violent winds, especially from the south-west, came sweeping round the foot of Salisbury Craigs, and rendered it, though laid out in those days with roads intended to be paths of pleasantness, forlorn and comfortless, except when the air was calm and mild! even then it was but little frequented, so that at all times it was a fit haunt for the moody meditations of revenge and disappointment. On the present occasion the two adventurers were the only persons within the enclosure, and each towards the other experienced the influence of the morose genius of the solitude.

They walked for some time without speaking. At last Chatelard, who was naturally more communicative, said—

"What think you, Rizzio, I ought to do? It might be attended with hazard, were I to attempt to evade the order to quit the kingdom to-morrow."

"It might be inconvenient," replied Rizzio, sedately; "but if the Queen regards you with

that distinction which is all the gossip of the Palace this morning, the risk is not such that a young man even of less spirit would hesitate to encounter."

In saying this the words were weighedly delivered, and the keen scrutiny of the Italian's dark eye made the secret thoughts and wishes of Chatelard shrink.

"We are strangers in this country, Rizzio, and the inhabitants do not endure our presence willingly. If we have not enemies we have adversaries, and therefore we should stand by one another. I beg you, therefore, to give me your best advice in my present difficulties."

"I cannot refuse you that, Chatelard; but to enable me to do so you must give me all your sincerest confidence, and by no concealment expose me to the responsibility of having advised you to adopt a course of conduct at variance with actual facts and circumstances."

The Frenchman assured him that there was nothing he would conceal, and that he was ready to answer every question.

"Then my first," said Rizzio, "will be a plain one."

There was a lurking exultation in the cunning eye of the Italian as he said this, and especially when he enquired if the Queen had ever, of her own disposition, given him any familiar token of partiality.

Chatelard reddened to crimson, and appeared to hesitate, which induced Rizzio to add—

" Come, you must deal candidly with me or let no more pass between us."

" She," said Chatelard, " has at my request granted Knockwhinnie's pardon."

" That," said Rizzio, drily, " certainly is something, and will be, as you have already experienced, considered great by many." He, however, thought to himself " this may have been conceded only to him as the last applicant; worn out by importunity, she may have merely accidentally then yielded what she was predisposed to grant;" and he resumed aloud—" But in granting Knockwhinnie's pardon on your intercession, she may have thought it would promote your suit with Adelaide, as it would secure to you, from her at least, some sentiment of gratitude."

Chatelard became confused, and, not evincing any disposition to reply, Rizzio said jocularly, but with a cast of sarcasm in his voice,

"Perhaps you don't much care for Adelaide? In truth, Chatelard, to be plain with you, there has been, I have sometimes thought, more of the tongue than of the heart, in the professions of your love for her. You may as well, therefore, out with the truth."

"Would you have me read a recantation? I will, however, tell you all. I have felt all the enchantments of the passion: but while I spoke of Adelaide, my fancy was engaged with another."

"I thought so," replied Rizzio; "and I think that other may be guessed at."

Chatelard was startled at hearing this. He had imagined that he had acted with so much dexterity and address, that no one could have detected his devotion to the Queen; for Love is not only blind to the defects of its object, but insensible to its own nakedness.

"But," continued Rizzio, "we lose time: you promised the confidence of a confession, and yet

you appear to keep only the promise to the ear. Come, come! there must be no evasion with me. You have been, ever since our voyage, up to the ears in love with the Queen."

"The Queen!" echoed Chatelard, with a sardonic laugh. "You take great freedom with her Majesty, to say so!"

"How! I did not say she was in love with you! Now the pith of your case lies there. It is a natural sentiment that a young man should be fascinated by such desirable beauty; but tell me now in what other way, than by Knockwhinnie's pardon, have you received from her any mark of preference?"

"I think," replied Chatelard, puzzled at being so closely pressed, "you have watched too well not to have discovered the pleasure she takes in hearing me sing?"

"Yes, you are an eloquent singer; there is no other so tasteful among all her musicians; but whether it was for yourself, or for your song, that you have been so frequent a guest at her suppers, might trouble a casuist to determine."

"While Rizzio was thus probing the bosom of the vain but unsuspecting Chatelard, his victim became more and more entangled in his coils.

"Have you had no other sign of preference than her delight in your melodies?"

"In sooth," said the Frenchman, "such tokens are not so palpable as to be made very obvious to third parties: but she hath always presented her hand to me. To no other of the guests at her familiar entertainments hath she ever vouchsafed the distinction."

"Hem! that is touching the matter more closely. Have you ever by accident been left alone with her?"

"Yes, several times, when my duty called me to consult the answers to be given to letters and missives from Rome and Paris."

"And what was her manner on such occasions?"

"Sometimes gracious and bland, encouraging me freely to speak my mind; but of late she hath much changed, and has been on such occasions reserved and ceremonious."

"Aye," said Rizzio; "that looks as if she had some knowledge of your affection, and would repress it; she therefore needs no declaration to tell her of the ardour with which you have been fired."

"I think so too; I cannot doubt it; for twice, when I have pressed her hand with tender eagerness, she hath snatched it away, conscious of the touch."

"Have you done so already? By my troth, Chatelard! you are nearer the consummation of your fortunes than I thought. I pray you, when you are master, to remember that I was once your friend. Seek no mediator with her; but find some opportunity to speak yourself for yourself. I see between you and great prosperity but the frail barrier of diffidence and modesty. Be you bold, and fear not her blushes. I know not that I can say more. Upon yourself depends your fortunes; and, believe me, let us henceforth not be seen too much or openly together. Yours is a task that but yourself can toil in; and let me say again, when you are master, forget not that we were once coequal and confiding friends. As

the wind has set this morning, be none surprised that you see me put on the mask of a changed look; be not offended at it. In sooth, Chatelard, were I in your shoes, let the wind blow high or low, I should not sail to-morrow for France, nor be many hours till I had thrown for the stake I play for."

Rizzio soon after left him, and Chatelard continued to walk in the solitary park alone. The occasional passer-by, who saw him ruminating there, and who had heard of his dismissal, moralized on the uncertain fortunes of those who put their trust in princes. But his ruminations were not of the pale hue of dejection; they were rich with the crimson of ambition: the insinuations of Rizzio had infected his vanity, and, like the ingredients of a sorcerer's spell, bewitched his imagination with dangerous illusions.

At first his mind ran riot; he fancied all the gorgeous and delightful visions of his intoxicated passion realized, and schemed, upon that supposition, as to the department he would assume in the state, and the vengeance he would inflict on

Dufroy, to whom alone he attributed his humiliation. This effervescence, however, soon subsided; and he found that much was to be done, before it could be in his power even to feel himself safe in remaining in Scotland. Access to the Queen was forbidden; and it was from herself alone that he could hope even for indulgence only to remain. Here the suggestion of the Italian's machination took effect; and he exclaimed, with some vehemence of gesture,

"I will see her! I will hazard something to attain an interview! The prize is immeasurable; and men of greater weight, without half of my motive, have not scrupled to hazard life in a meaner pursuit. I dally with my destiny, in allowing others to stand upon the vantage-ground against me."

Thus, in loose reflections, but not without aim, he continued his soliloquy, till, having wound himself up to the resolution of obtaining access to the Queen, he began to meditate on the means, and concluded, that by Knockwhinnie, and his influence with his daughter, it was not impossible he might ob-

tain admission into her Majesty's apartments. No time was to be lost in carrying this design into effect. The remainder of that day, and the night, was all he had left to accomplish it.

CHAPTER XXIII.

"Yet innocence and virgin modesty,
 Her virtue, and the conscience of her worth,
 That would be wooed, and not unsought be won."
                                                MILTON.

WE shall pass over the interview between Knockwhinnie and his daughter; but in doing so, it is not the Grecian's veil that we draw. There were no such circumstances in their mutual or respective feelings, to make this necessary. The one knew not the other, even by sight. It was only some undefinable deference for the opinion which the world holds of fatherly feelings and filial duties, that made their first meeting interesting. A few natural tears they shed, befitting the occasion; but we should do injustice to the candour of Adelaide's character, were we to describe her emotion as more than the homage of custom.

Knockwhinnie himself was delighted with his daughter. Who, indeed, had ever looked upon her without sentiments of pleasure? and yet it was a pleasure mingled with compassion, for her loveliness was pale and fragile; bespeaking by the simple elegance of her manners, protection and help. Her father could do no less than obey the influence of nature when he first beheld her: but she probably felt less than he did; for the generosity of the firm and calm Dufroy had prevented her from suffering the sorrow and the anxieties of the orphan condition, in which she had been left.

While they were together, Dufroy, not aware that Knockwhinnie was with her, entered her apartment with his accustomed freedom. We have already stated that he was influenced by a secret though not very strong anger against her father; and this, no doubt, had an influence on his demeanour towards him. Perhaps also, for we must speak of men as they are, the Count was not altogether well pleased at Knockwhinnie, merely from the manner in which his pardon had been obtained; for when the feelings have

once been ravelled, they are seldom ever afterwards restored to the simplicity of the natural skein. We should do wrong, however, to the high sentiments of that nobleman, were we to allege that he was absolutely disturbed at the pardon, as respected Knockwhinnie personally, although he considered it a manifestation of clemency inconsistent with public justice.

A cold dry interchange of recognition was all that took place between them. The Count congratulated Adelaide on the restoration of her father; and, with the expression of a few formal civilities, left them together.

The character of Knockwhinnie, from his wild and hunted life, had undergone an impressive change. In youth he had been distinguished for the courtly gallantry which was common to the young gentry of the country in those days; and he was naturally prompt in determination, and adventurous in action. He possessed also the best substance of the virtues connected with these attributes; but a long series of anxieties had made him susceptible to the slightest alarm; and he distrusted, more or less,

all with whom he had not been before, his outlawry well acquainted. Constant tribulation had made him irascible far beyond his constitutional temperament. A small matter, like a mote in the eye, afflicted him beyond his power of endurance; and had the effect of so corroding his milder qualities, that the friends who recollected him in the urbanity of his younger years, could hardly discern in the pardoned Outlaw the same individual whom they had formerly known. The change was not, however, of a vital nature; it was but an incrustation—the broken and rugged ice, under which the stream continued to flow in its natural purity—the snow, under which the power of vegetation suffered no diminution—the brown and rough clods, under which the seed was germinating with undiminished vigour. His manners were abrupt, but sensitive,—the effects of his perils and mischances: his sensibility however, an inherent quality, was contracted in quantity, if we may so say, and augmented in intensity. The elements of goodness were strong within him; and those who liked him least at first, liked him most in the end. It might be said,

which she had experienced from the Count Dufroy produced a strong impression. It could not at once extinguish the long-cherished animosity which he had entertained against him, but it disposed him, with the conviction of the Count's blamelessness, to wish he could better esteem that nobleman; and he said to Adelaide with warmth, that he would endeavour to prove how justly he valued the disinterested kindness with which he had so fostered and protected her.

In the course of conversation he spoke also with the warmth of grateful feelings for the obligation he owed to Chatelard, and assured Adelaide, that although, but for that service, he would have preferred Southennan; yet, if the young Frenchman was really disposed to accept her hand, it would be his study and delight to promote their happiness; and he concluded by saying it would be a false modesty on her part,

her attachment being so generally suspected, not to do all in her power to avert the execution of the sentence of expulsion which Dufroy had obtained against him.

In this advice there was doubtless the plain-dealing of a mind habituated to hasty decisions; but it was delicate and dignified in the gentle spirit of Adelaide to make no objection to the suggestion;

"I may never," said she, "obtain his love, but I can deserve his esteem."

Little did either father or daughter imagine, when arranging this blameless plot, in which gratitude and love were the only conspirators, that they were laying the foundations of a plan, by which he, whom they were so anxious to serve, would be utterly ruined.

In the meantime the Queen, much disturbed by the transactions of the morning, was dissatisfied with her own want of decision. She clearly perceived that she had done something wrong, not in the act itself, but from her own easiness of nature in the manner of doing it. She saw that, although she had yielded with

candour and even with alacrity to the advice of the Count Dufroy, whom she esteemed as her trustiest friend, in banishing Chatelard, that she had only furnished fuel to the beacons of detraction. She condemned herself for having, in a momentary fit of spleen, sacrificed, as she was sure it would be considered, her own dignity, and it was impossible to disguise to herself, that in consenting to dismiss Chatelard, and to drive him forth the kingdom, there was some acknowledgment of danger being in his presence. All her feelings were warped and disordered by this reflection. She wished it were possible to recal the mandate of expulsion, and merely to confine the penalty to the dismissal. But her orders had been published; she could not rescind them without giving fresh cause for suspicion, and she had endured both from her brother, the Prior of St. Andrew's, and the Earl of Morton, as well as other influential counsellors, both of the popish and reformed factions, austere admonitions for her weakness and irresolution. It may, therefore, be easily imagined, that after the departure of Knock-

whinnie, when Adelaide joined her Majesty, she was in no better state of mind to resist the application of Adelaide to mitigate the sentence of Chatelard, than she was to resist his application for the pardon of Knockwhinnie. Experience, however, of the inconvenience that might arise from the indulgence of generosity, had, in the course of the day, taught her to be less precipitate. She promised Adelaide to take her entreaty into consideration, and to use the best reasons in her power, to bring her confidential friends to acquiesce in the mitigation.

"Alas!" said she, "how little is it in the power of royalty, even to indulge itself in the desire to soften misfortune. O! my gentle Adelaide, I am not fit to withstand the cabals that surround me. Would it had pleased heaven to have cast my lot in a humbler sphere. I feel that, as an honoured gentlewoman, I could have dispensed and received happiness. But Heaven forfend me from the fulfilment of the omens which darken in the future! Whom have I to advise me? I am upon a pinnacle; every wind blows upon me; I cannot move

without the risk of falling; and for a queen to fall is never to rise again. Look all around; there is not one half so forlorn. You have a father and Dufroy; but from my childhood I have been a lonely orphan, and since I came ill-fated to this country, the aspect of every day has been more dismal than the past. But the daughter of a hundred kings will not shrink in her trials: honour, felicity, love, and renown, are never to be mine; but I feel an assurance in my heart, that the malice of adversity shall never subdue me!"

CHAPTER XXIV.

" What I can do I will."

OTHELLO.

WHILE the deep bass of court intrigue and machination was thus shaking the heart of the Sovereign, the shrill clear treble of lighter affairs was vibrating through the hearts of private individuals, and the appogiaturas of small afflictions increased the effect, without adding to the importance of Mistress Marjory's share in the diapason. She had never been able to reconcile herself to Southennan for the manner in which he rejected her proposition to accompany him to the Reception. She could not exactly, as any modern Edinburgh landlady may possibly have done, during the late royal visit, complain of him as an upstart. Looms were not in those days utterly unknown, but steam-engines and

spinning jennies were visions that had not dawned even in the prospective horizon of philosophical anticipation. Southennan, a scion of an ancient stock, was in all respects her equal, or rather her superior; but he was not altogether free, in her opinion, from blame. He had been in France, as she understood, and therefore ought to have known something of good manners; but he had been among the Englishers, whom every true Scotchwoman and Scotchman believed were, in those days, a sort of anthropophagi.

The effect of her antipathy made the dignified and pedigreed Mistress Marjory withhold the light of her countenance, as much as possible, from our hero, and in her confidential confabulations with her kinsman Auchenbrae, to expatiate on the indignities she had suffered. Unfortunately, however, her auditor was not in such matters particularly sympathetic. He certainly lamented with her the decay of courtly breeding in the country, the increasing presumption of the lower orders, and the sneaking disposition of the higher to court, not only one another

who had any thing to give, but to address themselves, "cap-in-hand," to the rabble. All these things, Mistress Marjory correctly observed, were signs that a mutation was going on, and it was clear to her, that the end would be confusion. Auchenbrae, though loose enough, God wot! both in patriotism and principle, was not exactly of this opinion, and he endeavoured to smooth her bristles by comforting her with the assurance, that the demolition of the monasteries would increase the consequence of the nobility, by driving out of competition with them, the mitred abbots, the lordly priors, and the other proud and pampered ecclesiastics, who like locusts, ate up the green blades of the pastures.

"Weel," said Mistress Marjory, as they were one afternoon discussing the controversy of the Reformation, and beheld through the north window of her parlour the religious house of Inchkeith in flames, "I never heard sic a sensible account o' the Reformation before; for between you and me, though in the way o' a peace-offering, the kirk allowed the Lazaruses o' the nobility to pick up the crumbs that fell

from her table, she ay keepit the main banquet for her ain children, the whilk I hae heard my grand-uncle, Lord Archibald, tell, would sooner or latter breed a feud in the realm, for it wasna' to be thought that the nobility and gentry would endure to see themselves coped wi' by sic a wiveless and bairnless herd o' a priesthood, that had nae other superiority but book-lear, and something that they call philosophy. Really, Auchenbrae, I'll be turning round too; but I fear its no ordained for womankind to get either a shave o' the loaf, or a slice o' the round."

Auchenbrae told her that he was much inclined to the same way of thinking.

"The only doubt I have," said he, "is, if they would refrain from persecuting me, even if I did turn reformer."

"That's a natural dubiety, Auchenbrae; and I would advise you to keep clear o' the fangs and teeth o' persecution as lang as ye can, for I misdoubt if ye're in a condition to be a martyr."

"Well," said he, "but tell me, my kind cousin, what I ought to do; for here am I chased and hunted like a fox, and lying hiding

in your house, to the great discomfort of yourself and the waste of victuals in your aumry. Have you no friend, cousin, at the Court that would soften the Queen's ear for my benefit?"

"Hech hey," replied Mistress Marjory; "as wealth wanders, worth weakens; wha could I speak to? My uncle, the Lord Archibald, is dead and gane, and my second cousin is only a laddie. I trust he'll mend in time! and there's need for't; for really he looks as if he would be never better than a sucking turkey."

"No doubt," rejoined Auchenbrae, "what you say is very true; but could not you put on your cockernonie and your cardinal, and go to your old friend the Earl of Morton, and make intercession for me; for though he is a gruesome carle, he is yet lightly won they say by ladies' charms; and I have heard the Queen can wind him round her finger."

"Hah, Auchenbrae, that was a benison ye should hae asked twenty years ago, when I was conjunc' wi' his Lordship; for ye ken he's baith kith and kin to us. Ah, Auchenbrae, I ha'e lost twa front teeth—mark o' mouth—its an undertaking I darena attempt."

"Had your adversary, Mistress Marjory, said so in my hearing, I'll not tell you what might have been the upshot; but you misliken your powers of pleasing. Sure am I you might do something for me with the Lord Morton. But if you think it is an impossibility, is not there past Bailie Brown, that still rules the Town Council; could not you try your pawkrie with him?"

"That," replied the lady, "needs nae putting up to; but his wife, ye ken, is sib to your auld adversary Knockwhinnie, against whom ye hae sworn a heavenly animosity, as if he were the Incarnated himself."

"Well," said Auchenbrae, with something between a grumble and a sigh, "my situation is more helpless than I thought. However, Mistress Marjory, as you are a lady both of gumption and talons, as I may say, I put my despair into your hands—worse it cannot be made; and, if it be possible, your friendliness may make it better. At present I am forlorn and useless."

Mistress Marjory, notwithstanding the jocular

vein in which Auchenbrae spoke, heard him with sorrow; but, like her sex, in the greatest straits she was not without resources. From the time that Southennan had become her lodger, she had held many sweet and precious communings with Father Jerome; she knew that he was a familiar and accepted coadjutor in the councils of the Abbot of Kilwinning; and she thought that possibly she might be able so to work with him as to procure his good will with the Abbot on behalf of her kinsman.

"No," said she, when she spoke to the holy Father on the subject, "that I think Auchenbrae, whom ye better ken as Friar Michael, is just an innocent lamb. He has his fau'ts; wha hasna' that's come o' gentle blood?—it's the very testification o' the purity o' his pedigree; but in the main he's a free jocose gentleman, and would be an honour to the Queen's Court, if he were a thought better schooled."

Father Jerome told her that he had a great friendship for Auchenbrae;

"But really," he added, "Madam, these are not times when either by fee or favour the

church should espouse malefactors. I have a great dread that Anchenbrae is one of that sort, and my Lord Abbot is minded never to let a black sheep again into our folds."

"I ay," replied the lady, "thought ye were a bye ordinar discreet man, and what ye hae said shows that ye're no void o' a' sagacity; but nae doubt, though it may no be a very comely thing for you to make or meddle in this matter wi' the Lord Abbot, surely ye might gie me a bit inkling o' what would be efficacious."

"Then," replied Father Jerome, " speak to our Laird; he has got a pith and power at the Court that's a perplexity to me."

"Your Laird!" exclaimed the lady, indignant at the proposition, all her wrath mounting into a blaze with the remembrance of the contumely with which he had treated her; " your Laird! would I ask him? I would sooner—but I'll no say what he is."

While they were thus speaking, Southennan came to the door, and was admitted by Hugboc.

"Oh, megsty Laird!" said the boy, " but ye're come in the nick o' time. Father Michael

is in this house, and has been keelevying wi' Mistress Marjory in her own chamber; and they, with the help o' Father Jerome's counsel, are plotting to tye an auld pan to your tail."

"How heard you this?" said Southennan, laughing.

"Od, ye see I'm a true and faithfu' servant, and I hae nae broo o' the folk o' this town; so I gaed to the key-hole, and put my e'e first, and syne my lug, to see and to hear what they were gallanting about; and when the leddy, after her exploit wi' Friar Michael, jooked out o' the room to Father Jerome, I gaed to hearken there likewise. Oh Laird! what a hard servitude I ha'e had ever since we came into this town; I never ha'e a right wink o' sleep on account o' the troubles o' my curiosity; and over and above all, our Baldy has just turned a demented creature. I dinna think, Laird, ye'll be able to thole wi' him long; and I'm sure ye'll no get a laddie that will be mair eydant than I ha'e been; and I'm a year aulder than when your father, the grand Laird Walter, made him his body servant."

Southennan was amused at the cunning and simplicity of the boy, and flattered his hopes and his vanity by telling him, that since they had come into Edinburgh he had certainly, both in adroitness and intelligence, surpassed his expectations.

CHAPTER XXV.

"I would I might entreat your honour
To scan this thing."

OTHELLO.

THE anxieties of the day, the steep streets, and Mistress Marjory's high stairs, had, in the words of the town-clerk, made our hero so "exhoust and forfoughten," that he required some recruiting stimulus, and accordingly gave orders to prepare a stoup of hippocras. When it was ready Baldy brought it into the room, leaving the door accidentally open, by which Hughoc was seen listening on the outside, concealed, but looking from time to time in.

"I'm thinking," said Baldy, as he placed the flaggon on the table, "that the Laird will find this savoury drink. I wish a' the Queen's lieges had as gude comfort. As for Knockwhinnie,

our auld fellow-traveller, he stands I'm thinking, but little in need o't. It's comfort enough in a'e day for an outlaw to get his pardon. He's well off; but Auchenbrae's to be pitied; hunted to the ends of the earth as if he were na'e better than a tod lowry. Will the drink do?"

Hughoc during this speech looked in from the lobby, and shook his forefinger in an admonitory manner to his master.

Baldy continued,

"Some folks say, Laird, that ye ha'e been instrumental in getting Knockwhinnie's pardon, and I'll no deny that ye may therein ha'e done a merciful almous; but surely a man that would take anither's life wi' cauld iron, is a far blacker malefactor than a free-hearted gentleman giving a slap on the back wi' only the butt end o' his whip to a doited carle, tho' he was birsling his shins at his ain fire-side. If I might be sae bold, Laird, I would make an intercession for a help o' your hand to relieve Auchenbrae."

Hughoc had stepped full in front of the door, and when he heard this he raised his hands, and looked with amazement, as if each particular ori-

fice in his countenance had been an organ of sight. His master could not, without a struggle, prevent himself from laughing at the droll physiognomy of the boy, and Baldy, seeing the smile struggling through, attributed it to the progress of compassion and sympathy.

"I'm sure, Laird," said he, "ye'll no refuse the sma' favour o' interceding wi' the Queen's Majesty for Auchenbrae. I dinna say he's a clear innocent man; but far waur' than him ha'e before now been spared to a gude auld age without fear o' the wuddy."

Hughoc could not stand this; so he came into the room, and lifting the flaggon with the hippocras, not knowing what other pretext to make for his intrusion, carried it off.

"What do you mean by that? come back with it!" exclaimed Southennan.

Hughoc replaced it on the table, and looking with the fierceness of a terrier at Baldy, sullenly retired to the lobby again.

"That laddie," said Baldy, "is either gaun aff at the head, or growing a Protestant; for he has nae mair reverence for me now, sic is the

corruption o' the court and the city, than if I were a broom besom. Wherever I gang, if he's no on duty wi you, he follows me like a messin, and lays his lug to every word that's said, just like a filler in the mouth o' a Rotterdam greybeard; nae drap, nae word of speech can fa' past it."

The wrath of Hugboc at this backbiting was neither to hold nor to bind; he sprung into the room, and shaking his fist at Baldy, said, "Ah, ye crab, ye lering scouther! Ye 're a black neb."

Southennan, to keep peace ordered the boy to retire, and to shut the door, and to show more respect to his elder. This decision was duly appreciated by Baldy, who proceeded to urge more and more distinctly and decidedly the kindness that would be conferred by procuring remission of Auchenbrae's offence.

It appeared to Southennan somewhat extraordinary, that Baldy, so much of a sudden, should have interfered so strongly on behalf of Auchenbrae, especially as he well knew that their acquaintance was very slight indeed, and

that Knockwhinnie, his own particular friend (for by this time he so considered him), had been vitally injured by that delinquent. Doubtless the reports which Hughoc had made of the intrigues of Baldy and Father Jerome had not been without effect on his mind, and he recollected also with some degree of heat, that he was supposed to be circumvented by his servant. He, however, said nothing, but allowed Baldy to finish his exhortation, at the end of which he looked at him steadily, and then said, with unusual emphasis,

" You have been long a faithful servant in my family; but you must not attempt to render me subservient to any plan in which you are concerned, whether it be for religion, policy, or interest. I will not interfere on behalf of Auchenbrae, and you will remember never to speak in his behalf to me again."

Baldy instantly retired, and presently a yelling was heard in the house, caused by the crusty old man indemnifying himself for the reproof he had received at the expense of Hughoc. Soon after, Baldy went out, and the time being near

when the frequenters of the Unicorn were in the practice of assembling in the evening, Souththennan went to join them. On entering the room he was surprised, and uneasily so, at seeing Knockwhinnie and Chatelard sitting together, seemingly in serious confidential conversation. He was still more struck on perceiving, that when they observed him they changed their topic, and addressed him as if they intended he should think there was nothing particular in the matter of their whispered discussion. Among other guests who subsequently came in was Rizzio, whose air and demeanour towards Chatelard surprised him still more. It had never occured to him, that there had been any such misconduct in the cause of Chatelard's dismissal as to impose a change in the manner of his friends; but Rizzio was conspicuously reserved, and scarcely seemed to recognise him. His look was so dry and cold, that he seemed as if he had endured some offence at his hands; indeed, his whole behaviour was so estranged, that it repressed the wish which our hero felt to inquire what occurrence had so ruptured their former intimacy.

"On the part of Chatelard the alienation was not so obvious; but he seemed to feel no annoyance at the manner in which he was treated by Rizzio; on the contrary, he appeared not only as if he were acquainted with the cause, but that he attached no importance to it. Indeed, he so far appeared to forget it that, in the course of a few minutes, he rose and attempted to take hold of Rizzio's arm in his old familiar manner; but the Italian turned sharply round, and with an impressive look, made him desist. In this there was something so like mystery that it did not satisfy our hero; and he could not resist the suspicion of some arrangement having been secretly concerted between them. Nor after the crafty conversation which he had held on the preceding day with the Italian in the same room, was it without warranty.

Chatelard having resumed his seat beside Knockwhinnie, Southennan joined Rizzio, and inquired, in a friendly tone, what had happened to cause so great a change in his demeanour towards the Frenchman.

"The nature of Chatelard's imputed

fence," said he, "renders it necessary that the confidential servants of the Queen should separate themselves entirely from him; it may else be supposed that we have been privy to his presumption, and ought to have informed the Chancellor, or the Prior of St. Andrews, of what we had observed."

Southennan stepped back in astonishment at this ex post facto prudence, and said,

"How is this? You observed how much he was enamoured of the Queen as early as I did, and the fault of concealment has already been committed."

The Italian, not being well prepared for this home-thrust, looked confused.

"Come, come," exclaimed Southennan, "no masquerading with me; there is something going on between you. I hope it has no other object than to procure his restoration to the Queen's service."

Rizzio bit his lips with vexation; for the deepest cunning cannot always provide against the plain dealing of simplicity and honour. His answer, however, was firmly delivered, and was irresistibly plausible.

"Until it has been seen how such things thrive, it is not wise to blab of what one may know. Had Chatelard prospered in his bold passion, where should I have been now, had I betrayed my suspicions; for after all they were but suspicions. Courts are epitomes of the world; nothing is bad in them until it is known. The Spartan law is that also of all courts—it is the discovery that makes the crime; and I would advise you, as a candidate for public employments, to study the lesson."

This speech grated the hearing of Southennan, and made him feel something like distaste against Rizzio. He had often before experienced the same repugnance, but in this instance it was tinctured with dread, and he was awed by the too evident craft and capacity of his character.

While they were speaking apart, Knockwhinnie and Chatelard left the room somewhat abruptly together. Their evasion was, no doubt, intended to appear an incidental occurrence, but it was done in such haste and hurry, that it attracted the attention of several

gentlemen, and occasioned a temporary suspension of their conversation.

Rizzio, whose quick eye allowed nothing to escape unobserved, said—

" What has so suddenly affected your friends? They appear to have been roused on the instant to some undertaking, and it is a grave one; for neither of them have art of countenance enough to hide the indications of their thoughts. It cannot be that Knockwhinnie has consented to give him his daughter?"

This suggestion was so much in unison with the apprehensions of our hero, that it seemed as probable as it was alarming. Finding himself in consequence unable to conceal his emotion, he turned round to Cornylees, who had just entered, and taking him by the arm, requested him to walk into the air with him, as the room was close, and it was yet a full half-hour to supper time.

CHAPTER XXVI.

"Good things of day begin to droop and drouze,
And evil things themselves do rouze."

The subject of the conversation of Knockwhinnie with Chatelard was an effect of the suggestions of Rizzio in the Park. The Frenchman was determined to make an effort to see the Queen; he had but that night left to accomplish his purpose, and when Knockwhinnie was expressing his sorrow in being the unconscious cause of his dismissal, he adroitly represented, that if he could possibly obtain an audience of her Majesty, he was convinced that he would be immediately reinstated in his employments.

Knockwhinnie had as yet heard but few particulars of the story. The representation was

plausible, and he voluntary proposed that they should at once proceed to the palace, and endeavour, by the means of Adelaide, to obtain a secret interview with her Majesty. This occasioned their sudden departure from the Unicorn.

On reaching Holyrood House, Chatelard, who was acquainted with the private passages and back stairs, conducted Knockwhinnie to the special apartment of Adelaide, and they deemed themselves fortunate in finding her there alone.

At their entrance she was in tears; and when she saw Chatelard with her father she uttered a faint and feeble shriek, which sufficiently indicated the cause and the subject of her sorrow.

Her father began to relate the purpose of their visit by reiterating the obligations for which he was indebted to Chatelard, and to lament that it had been visited by such fatal consequences to himself.

"There is," said Knockwhinnie, "no other alternative but for him to see the Queen; he is persuaded that she will remit the dismissal; at all events allow him to remain in Scotland, and then"—

He smiled on Chatelard, and taking the hand of Adelaide, presented it to him; but to his surprise, she hastily withdrew it.

"How can I comply with your request," said Adelaide to her father, "without offending the commands of her Majesty, and incurring the reproach of the Count, who would regard such disobedience as dishonourable."

The mention of Dufroy's name, and in that manner, stung Knockwhinnie, and he replied with some degree of severity—

"Is it thus that you obey your newly found father?"

Adelaide made no reply, but said to Chatelard—

"I doubt if the Queen will receive you as you expect. Be not deceived; she has been subjected to remonstrance on your account already. Why do you hope that your application will have more weight than another's with her? I cannot comply with my father's request; but I will go to her Majesty, and solicit her grace for you with all the earnestness in my power."

This firmness in the mild and maidenly Adelaide, checked the answer that her father intended to return, and sitting down he told her that they would wait till she came back.

The room was hung with tapestry, as we have already described, exhibiting the parting of Dido and Æneas. As Knockwhinnie looked at it by the light on the table, it seemed to him to represent some similitude to the crisis in which the fortunes of Chatelard and his daughter then stood, and he continued looking at the picture for some time without speaking.

Instead of proceeding to the Queen's apartment by the door which communicated with the gallery, Adelaide lifted a corner of the arras, behind which was a door that led to the Queen's bed-chamber, where her Majesty was then dressing for the evening. With this concealed entrance Chatelard was not before acquainted, and he looked at it so eagerly when it was opened, that Knockwhinnie encouraged him to follow Adelaide; but he at that time durst not venture; it was a step too bold; but the advice was not lost upon him; for although

it was not exactly to the same effect as the insidious suggestions of Rizzio, it was yet in accordance with their spirit. Adelaide was not long absent; her mission had failed; the Queen interrupted her in the very overture and exordium of her solicitation, and declared that she had been so offended by the presumption of Chatelard, that she would no longer permit his name to be repeated in her presence. Adelaide communicated this with considerable emotion; but she concealed that she had been chided by the Queen for having so far forgot her native modesty in undertaking the mediation; for she had not thought it requisite to mention how she had been urged by her father.

It being now the hour when the Queen's evening circle was formed, Adelaide was obliged to to leave them, and it was perhaps fortunate for herself that the claim of duty denied the opportunity of a formal farewell. She felt indeed that it would be a scene more trying than she could, with becoming propriety, support, and accordingly she hastily returned to the Queen, leaving her father and Chatelard together. From the

moment of her exit the Frenchman became evidently restless and impatient, until they had left the apartment.

The door which communicated with the private stairs by which they had ascended, could only be secured by a bolt and staple on the inner side. Chatelard had remarked this, but it escaped the observation of Knockwhinnie. The thoughts which, in the meantime, were passing in the mind of the Frenchman, were soon manifested. In leaving the apartment he contrived that Knockwhinnie should precede him, and he affected, when he came out, to be particular in closing the door. The darkness of the staircase facilitated his stratagem.

They then returned to the Unicorn, and reached the door as Rizzio was coming out. Full of his intent, but not daring to breathe it, Chatelard looking significantly and exultingly, pressed him by the hand in silence as he passed. The hint, however, was sufficient; the Italian, without much reflection, conjectured that somehow, by the mediation of Adelaide, the pre-doomed young man was to obtain access to the Queen.

In the meantime Southennan and Cornylees had strolled towards the Palace; and the former, without assigning any reason for not returning to supper, though the Laird was hungry and importunate, lingered round the precincts till he saw Chatelard and Knockwhinnie returning. He then affected compliance with the impatience of Cornylees; but soon after meeting Rizzio, he stopped to speak with him, and allowed the Laird to proceed alone.

The manner of Rizzio was now already altered; he was eager, vivacious, and excited. He requested, nay, insisted on Southennan returning with him to the Palace; he even expressed something like a congratulation that he was soon likely to be successful in his love; his whole manner, and even the sound of his voice, betokened extreme animation; insomuch that, although our hero repressed his inclination to inquire what had put him into such spirits, he could not resist his curiosity to see on what account Rizzio so earnestly, at that unwonted hour, sought his company.

On ascending the great stairs, Rizzio begged Southennan to remain in the gallery.

"I shall," said he, "only pay my homage, and return to you. Something will probably take place this evening, that may change the colour of Chatelard's condition. I wish you, therefore, to wait, that you may see in what the event will come to pass."

He then left Southennan in the gallery, where a number of gentlemen, not that night admitted to the presence, were playing at cards and chess. Without attaching himself to any party, our hero sat down and overlooked the card-players. Rizzio, however, did not return so soon as he expected, and he began to think with himself that it was useless to remain much later. In this notion he was confirmed by one of the gentlemen of the chamber coming from her Majesty; and who remarked that he had never seen her look more beautiful, nor in happier spirits, adding, that it would probably be late before she retired.

Southennan, on hearing this, gave up all hope of seeing Rizzio again, and descended into the court to return home; but as he was crossing to the portal he saw the shadow of a man

pass on the wall from a lamp which hung within a door that happened to be then open. Though it was but a shadow, which glided in a moment away, there was something in the contour of the figure that led him to fancy it was Chatelard. Without waiting, however, to ascertain the fact, he proceeded to the Unicorn, where, as he expected, he found Knockwhinnie and Cornylees engaged with a flask of Balwham's old sherries before them, discussing some important point concerning Cornylees' horse which he was disposed to sell, and for the same reason that he had offered his velvet suit for sale.

"Man Knockwhinnie," said he, "in course now, ye sall ha'e the braw beast for little mair than the wind o' your mouth. I wouldna' ha'e parted wi' it for twice the double o' the siller, but my purse has had, ever since I came to Embro', a severe bowel complaint; in course now, frae making owre free wi' the Maister Balwham's dainties and in fairings to the latherons in the Cowgate."

Southennan joined them, and a fresh flask

was opened; but he had scarce taken a glass, when Knockwhinnie, looking round the room, expressed his surprise at the disappearance of Chatelard, which recalled to Southennan's mind the shadow he had seen, and induced him to return to the Palace before the flask was finished, drawn as it were thither by some inscrutable attraction.

CHAPTER XXVII.

" Ring the alarum bell!"
MACBETH.

WHEN Southennan left the Unicorn, he was met by Hughoc, with a horn bowet in his hand, come, according to nightly custom, to conduct his master home in safety through the nocturnal "flowers of Edinburgh," which about that hour perfumed the ambient air, amidst the nightingale sounds of *gardez l'eau*, and the dashing of falling waters.

Edinburgh has probably been reformed in that indifferently since those days, and in the lapse of ages may reform it altogether; still we doubt if, with all the improvements in the High-street, any increase has been given to its picturesque effect when glimmeringly lighted up, as it then was by bowets and the moonlight.

The houses were of lath and plaster, white washed, and the cross beams painted black. Innumerable tall gables rose, crested with vanes and balls; and huge balconies, like the stern galleries of a Dutch man-of-war, projected over the street. When the moon shone bright, the effect of the black and white tenements was almost ghastly in the silence of the night, and the dim small wicks, that rather illuminated than shone from the horn lanterns, and which had only a short time before been introduced, proved how ineffectual they were for their trust.

Our hero on this occasion dispensed with his boy's attendance, and bade him return home, as he was going to the Palace, and might there be detained late.

" What ! " said Hughoc to himself as he was ascending towards the Cross, " what can he hae to do at the Palace at sic an untimeous hour ? I wish a' may be gaun right wi' the Queen and the Government. I would like to ken ! If I want my sleep, what will the master be the waur o' the sacrifice ? Od, I 'll gang down to the Palace

too, and the guard will let me sit in the guardhouse; for I'll let them see my bowet, and just say I'm come to bide for my master."

He accordingly turned round, and was snug in a corner of the guard-house before Southennan had well resumed his place beside the card-players in the gallery, where he had not long been when, much to his surprise, Knockwhinnie made his appearance.

Southennan affected not to observe him. He had not indeed, that day been much satisfied with the abrupt partiality with which he had attached himself to Chatelard. It seemed as if he had forgotten his warm professions of regard, and was exclusively interested in the Frenchman.

Whether Knockwhinnie noticed him or not, he did not approach him; for after passing twice up and down the gallery, as if in quest of some person, he went away.

Scarcely had he quitted the gallery, when a bustle and noise was heard in the Queen's apartments; the folding doors were thrown open, and the guests, all joyous and in high

glee, came out from her Majesty's presence. A short time elapsed before Rizzio appeared, and when he came his countenance was clouded with dark anxiety, strangely different from the general cheerfulness of the company.

On seeing Southennan he came directly to him, and proposed, as the night was fine, that they should move down into the open air; but Southennan, in the hope that Adelaide would pass through the gallery, and might afford him an opportunity of speaking to her, declined the proposal. Nothing could be more natural or sincere than the manner in which he objected to the proposition; but it would seem that Rizzio thought otherwise; for he looked at him with a sinister and apprehensive eye.

At that moment Adelaide came into the gallery, leaning on the arm of the Count Dufroy. She was evidently dejected, and seemingly not disposed to linger with the rest of the guests, but Southennan went forward and addressed her. A light conversation took place on different topics, in which no allusion was made to Chatelard's affair; but when the Count

conducted her to the door of her apartments, he said, after she had passed in,

"Have you seen anything of Chatelard?"

Southennan answered, by relating that he had been at the Unicorn, which he left some time before him.

"Do you know where he proposed to lodge to-night?" inquired the Count.

"Did you desire to see him, my Lord; for, although I do not know, yet as he was last with Knockwhinnie, I can easily learn."

"Oh no!" said the Count; "only it has been forgotten to be ascertained if he has been furnished with money for his voyage. I would, therefore, be glad to send him a supply if I knew where."

At this juncture, Southennan observed the door of Adelaide's apartments open, and herself, with a degree of wildness in her gaze, look out. She instantly, however, withdrew; and the door was shut. It would seem that Rizzio had also noticed this; for he went straight to the door, where he stopped, seemingly in a reverie, tracing characters with his finger on the panel; but

Southennan suspected, from the manner in which he once or twice inadvertently leaned with his ear to the door, that he was listening.

The company in the meantime were dispersing; and in the course of a few minutes, only Rizzio, the Count, and Southennan, remained in the gallery. The Count was in the act of bidding them good night, when the door was again opened, and Adelaide, in still greater terror, looked out. Seeing the company had departed, she came rushing to them, and threw herself, almost in a state of insensibility, into the arms of her adopted father.

"What has alarmed you? What has happened?"

She related, that she had found her room had been entered, and told him that she had been visited by her father; but she concealed that Chatelard had been there with him.

"The intruder," said she, "has entered by the private door; but nothing has been stolen. Every thing is as I left it."

Rizzio, on hearing this, went into the room, and examined it carefully. He was not ac-

quainted with the secret passage which led to the Queen's bed-chamber; but, finding the arras which hung over the door fluttering in a current of wind, lifted it aside, and saw the passage open. He inquired of Adelaide if she had been acquainted with it before; to which she readily answered in the affirmative; adding, that she had been through it to the Queen in the course of the evening.

The Count made light of the story. He said she deserved her fright; for he had no doubt that she had herself to blame for neglecting to fasten the door.

" But some one has been there!" she cried; " and one that has come hastily up from the court below. The prints of his footsteps are on the floor."

Rizzio at this moment returned to the group, and said,

"There has been certainly some one in the room—a man; and he has passed into the passage which leads to the Queen's chamber; but there is no trace that he has yet returned."

" Does any other," said the Count, " know of this passage ?"

The question ought not to have troubled Adelaide; but it did; and she was agitated to a great degree, when she replied,

" My father saw me go in to her Majesty, and return."

" It is strange!" said Rizzio, thinking aloud; and, like the other two, he at once concluded that the visit of her father was connected with the incident of her going to the Queen.

Count Dufroy made no remark, but led her back into her own apartment, and returned to the two gentlemen.

" Southennan," said he, " your Scottish air breeds craft. Here is this lovely and ingenuous creature already as adroit at intrigue as the chambermaid of a dowager. I have made light of this matter seemingly; but I suspect her father, out of a proper-enough feeling for the service he has obtained by Chatelard, has persuaded her to disregard the injunctions of her Majesty, and to plead for the imprudent and reckless young man. But her father would

not have ventured to intrude upon the Queen's privacy—into her bed-chamber. The thing is incredible!"

"I think so," replied Rizzio. "Moreover, the footstep is that of a smaller man than Knockwhinnie; and the alarm of Adelaide proves that she is convinced the intruder was some other than her father."

Southennan, during this colloquy, said nothing. He had no doubt that Chatelard had been there, and had been with Knockwhinnie during the time they were absent from the Unicorn together. He was convinced also, that the shadow he had seen was really Chatelard's; and recollecting the brief visit which Knockwhinnie had paid to the gallery, he was inclined to think the Frenchman was still concealed within the apartment. Just at this crisis, a loud screaming was heard from the ladies who were with the Queen. Adelaide came again rushing from her room, into which, sword in hand, the Count instantly ran, and proceeded through the secret passage to the Queen's chamber; whilst Rizzio and Southennan also, with swords drawn, hur-

ried through the public rooms to the same spot. Adelaide, in dreadful agitation, sank upon the floor; and the alarm spreading, the gallery was almost instantly filled with the guards, and with servants bearing lights and torches.

CHAPTER XXVIII.

"In what particular thought to work, I know not;
But in the gross and scope of my opinion,
This bodes some strange eruption to our state."
                                                HAMLET.

On entering the Queen's bed-chamber, they found her Majesty undressed, and her ladies surrounding her, extending their mantles to conceal her from view. In a corner of the room Chatelard stood overwhelmed with consternation: just as her Majesty was stepping into bed he had been discovered.

The amazement of Count Dufroy and Southennan was indescribable. Rizzio, however, was as collected and self-possessed as if he had been previously acquainted with the treason. The Queen herself was pale and alarmed; some of her ladies were of course screaming at the top of their voices, and others were shaking in every

limb like the aspen. The Count, before taking any step, looked stedfastly round the room; and then said to her Majesty, with a parental severity,

"Madam, what is your pleasure with respect to this gentleman?" pointing to Chatelard.

The Queen replied, "Let him be removed from this room; and let the Council be called, and determine concerning him."

By this time, all the adjoining rooms and passages were filled with the guards and men-at-arms. The Count summoned four of them to conduct the prisoner to the strong-room belonging to the guard; and dispatched messengers to call the Lords of the Council together. He then said to her Majesty that he would attend her pleasure when she was pleased to summon him; and withdrew with Southennan and Rizzio.

His behaviour during this remarkable scene was decided, even to sternness; he was performing what he felt to be a severe public duty: but there was a tone of melancholy and a cast of sadness in his manner, affecting and impressive in the few words which he addressed to the

Queen. His emotion was evident to every one, even in the turbulence of the confusion: but the painful sentiment by which he was actuated did not appear until he was at the door of the apartment. He there paused and sighed; a momentary hesitation detained him on the spot, but his wonted firmness was immediately recovered, and he went back to where the ladies were standing, and approaching with the customary public reverences to royalty, he took hold of the hand of Adelaide and brought her away. This action could not be mistaken; it produced an instantaneous solemnity: and the Queen, in great agitation, cried to him to remain in attendance, and she would presently see him. He retired from her as respectfully as he had advanced, and conducted his adopted daughter to his own apartment, without speaking; where he left her, saying,

" For this night I shall find a chamber for myself in another part of the Palace. To-morrow," said he, sorrowfully, " we shall pass from under this roof; and, if your father does not prohibit the intention, I will conduct you to

the old Countess of Kilburnie, your grandmother."

Adelaide, during the whole time, was incapable of making any reply; she was engrossed with unutterable fears and apprehensions. The detection of Chatelard in the Queen's bedchamber, overwhelmed her with feelings scarcely less dreadful than horror; and it was not until the Count had retired, and a flood of tears had come to her relief, that she was able to form any correct conception of the alarm and consternation which still shook the Palace.

The Count, after quitting Adelaide, returned to the gallery, from which the crowd had dispersed; only Rizzio and Southennan remained.

"What think you, gentlemen," said he, as he approached them, "of this humiliating transaction?"

"That the Queen has had no hand in it," replied Rizzio, alertly.

"And I think so too," rejoined Southennan.

"Then there must have been some incitement or instigation," said the Count; "an attempt so

audacious could not have been undertaken without encouragement!"

In saying this, he looked so sharply, that the Italian could not withstand the searching of his eye.

It was now sufficiently manifest that the Count suspected the purity of the Queen; but no word escaped from him, which in any degree could be construed to imply that opinion. While they were thus standing together — speaking abruptly at intervals, which showed how much their thoughts were engrossed with the occurrence, the Lady Mary Livingstone came through the apartments of Adelaide from the Queen, to request the attendance of the Count; a summons which he immediately obeyed, leaving that young lady with the two gentlemen.

No sooner had Dufroy left the gallery, than the whole appearance of Rizzio seemed to undergo a transformation; his mien became buoyant, and an irrepressible exultation shone as it were in his looks and gestures. He even ventured to jest with the lively Mary Livingstone, who did not seem to think there was any reason

touching life or death in the business; but the levity with which both Rizzio and this arch lady treated the adventure was not infectious: on the contrary, Southennan listened to their ill-timed gaiety with distaste. He saw by the manner in which Count Dufroy had been affected, that it was an adventure far more serious than they imagined.

When the Count entered to the Queen's presence he found her alone. Her appearance denoted extreme anxiety, a steady intense feeling, which showed itself in her features and air, but was unaccompanied with any visible emotion.

"I cannot," said her Majesty to him, "but discern that you believe me to have been privy and consenting to this most derogatory transaction."

The Count seemed on the point of returning some answer, but suddenly checking himself, he made a profound bow.

"I," resumed the Queen, "I am not surprised that you should put such a construction on it, because the matter of Knockwhinnie's

pardon, and other instances of the license which the unhappy young man has allowed himself to take, justify your suspicions. But———," and she rose from her seat, "I neither have forgotten my delicacy nor my dignity. I do not now order Chatelard to quit the kingdom, but you will convey to the Chancellor my determination, that his conduct shall be subjected to the utmost rigour of the law," and she cast her eyes with something like entreaty as she said, with undiminished serenity, " verily, Count! it is a cruel trial to the feminine heart to visit with ignominy one whose only offence has been in forgetting the Queen in a passion for the woman."

The Count emphatically said that her commands should be executed, and withdrew.

No incident hitherto in the life of this beautiful and accomplished Princess, had ever penetrated her bosom with so harsh an anguish as the lofty and ceremonious deportment of Dufroy on this occasion. She saw him leave the room with every wish to have recalled him; but, conscious of her innocence, and indignant to be so suspected, she remained as immovable as a sta-

tue. In this situation she was found by Lady Mary Livingstone, who returned from the gallery as the Count re-entered it.

"Who were the other gentlemen," said the Queen, "that came with the Count when the alarm was given?"

"Rizzio and Southennan."

"Livingstone," replied the Queen, "I am troubled. I dread that this unseemly adventure will come to some bloody issue. I cannot be merciful in this instance, without detriment to my honour, and sanctioning the infectious breath of slander. Go and bid Southennan come to me. He was a witness, and I would learn from himself what impression the discovery has made upon him; and come you back with him."

When Southennan approached her presence, her manner towards him was less marked, and she said, with much of her natural affability and condescension, that she had sent to inquire whether he had observed anything during the alarm, to give him reason to suppose that any of her attendants were privy to the intrusion.

The answer was satisfactory, and when he

mentioned the suspicion which the shadow had suggested, and the circumstance of Chatelard having been probably with Knockwhinnie when Adelaide had visited her Majesty before supper, she eagerly seized him by the hand, and cried,

"You have saved my honour."

This was the feminine impulse of the moment; for she immediately dropped his hand, and retiring a pace or two, desired him to send in Rizzio.

The rank which the Italian held in her household previous to this time, afforded him but few opportunities of addressing her. She knew that he was esteemed a young man of superior talent; she had often heard the acutest of her counsellors mention this; but the restricted etiquettes of the court had hitherto kept him at a distance.

She asked him the same questions which she had put to Southennan, and his answers were equally decisive. He mentioned what he had observed of the footsteps in the passage, and that he had conjectured they were those of Chatelard before the alarm was given. While

he was stating this, she fixed upon him the fascination as it were of her eye, and enquired if he thought she had been accessary to what had taken place.

Rizzio, with perfect truth, assured her that he had no such suspicion; that although he had often observed the impassioned ardour with which Chatelard had dared to regard her Majesty, he yet on no one occasion had ever remarked that she evinced any partiality for him. She expressed her satisfaction with the clearness of his recollections, and remembering the opinion she had often heard expressed of his sagacity and intelligence, she inquired in what way he thought she ought to act in the affair. This was a mark of confidence which, however much he longed for, he did not then expect; but he was ready with his answer, which he delivered with some method, and more than his usual address.

He alluded to her personal condition, to her youth, to the admiration with which she was contemplated, and to the rough and turbulent age in which she was placed, with exquisite deli-

cacy; comparing her to a fair bark in a turbulent sea, and a bright star amidst the clouds of a storm, and concluded with advising her not to interfere beyond the strict necessity of regal duty in Chatelard's affair. " Your Majesty," he concluded, " can only hope for tranquil enjoyment and a happy reign by uniting yourself to some eminent Prince, who will share the cares and the masculine duties of the sovereignty."

All this was so discreetly and so flatteringly delivered, that Mary blamed herself for having known so little of him before, and from that moment she resolved to consider him as one of her confidential advisers.

CHAPTER XXIX.

" Old men and beldames, in the streets
Do prophesy upon it dangerously."
SHAKSPEARE.

THE machination of Rizzio had thus succeeded; but after leaving the Queen's presence he did not feel " his bosom's lord sit lighter on his throne" by the event. It was his first crime: and although his friendship for Chatelard was not of that generous nature which was likely to have awakened much compunction for the double part he had played against him, he yet could not disguise from himself that no honourable heart could approve the craft of his incitements. Conscience acknowledged the guilt.

When he returned into the gallery he found a numerous assemblage of persons there, and that the Council was in deliberation; but he

kept himself aloof, and walked about as if in quest of something which he had lost and could not recover. He had, indeed, reached a point of fortune from which he might attain renown and power; but he found it was a headland, and that the prospect beyond it was crossed with black shadows and rugged chasms of many unknown dangers. The road he was to travel was rough, and the region through which it lay ominous with the unblest monuments of many victims.

The mind of Chatelard, at that time, as compared with Rizzio's, was as the mist in the calm to the wrack in the storm. His dread of punishment was soothed with the fallacious imagination that he was beloved by the Queen; and he stood, in consequence, in the presence of the Council, though perturbed and pale, cheered by this secret persuasion. It were tedious to recapitulate the circumstances of his examination. The fact of his treason in being discovered at an untimely hour in the Queen's bed-chamber, admitted of no extenuation; nor could the counsellors doubt the intent which had drawn him there.

"My lords," said the Earl of Morton, with his characteristic familiarity, when the examination was finished, "my lords, we shouldna' make twa bites of a cherry. That the hempie was found aneath the Queen's bed is proven; but that shews no *animus*. Now, unless we can make out what he was doing there, I canna' see wherein the treason lies; for surely, as some of your Lordships weel ken, its no sic a miraculous thing to catch a lad hidden in a young woman's chamber. My word, the fallow has a gude taste. But to speak in a solemn manner, as reverence for the Queen's Majesty requires we should do, I think he might hae been there by an accident. Wha can gainsay that? Or he might hae been looking for a curiosity, and hearing the Queen and her giggling leddies coming in, might hae crept in aneath the bed out o' sight, to make his escape at a mair convenient season. 'Deed, my lords! though no man can respec' the observance of a strict morality more than I do, yet this is a question that has twa sides, and it behoves us to take care in doing justice that we dinna' offend the Queen. My mind, and I hae had in my

day some preeing of human nature and of womankind, is an opinion, that we maybe would best consult discretion if we remitted the whole tot of the concern to be dealt with by her Majesty as in her wisdom and chastity she may see fit."

At this declaration the Count Dufroy addressed the Chancellor, and informed him of the injunctions he had received from the Queen to deal in this affair with the most rigorous adherence to the law."

"Weel," said Morton, "that changes my opinion. I doubt, Monsieur Chatelard, ye're in a bad way; for, as ye didna' please her Majesty, we, as ye hae heard, can do naething mair for your gude than to send you to the hangman; and in the meanwhile ye'll get every thing to make you comfortable."

The Prior of St. Andrews, who never much relished the gritty humour of the Earl, interposed, and said, that although no question could be raised as to the guilt of the prisoner, it was yet necessary, for the vindication of the Queen's honour, that he should be publicly brought to trial.

"My word, Jamie Stuart," said Morton, "I'll no say that thou's like the tod's whelp 'a day aulder a day waur;' but as the moon wanes thy wit waxes, and though we may be fashed wi' a trial, yet I agree that, for fashion's cause, we canna well put the varlet out of pain without the benefit of an advocate as well as an executioner; and therefore I move that he be sent to trial according to law."

The prisoner was then removed again to the strong-room, and the Council rising, passed into the gallery, where there was a great bustle in consequence of the Provost and the Town Council coming to address her Majesty on her escape from what they denominated "a rampant traitor."

"My Lord Provost," said the Earl of Morton jocularly, "ye should hae been sure, before ye came wi' your comforting condolence, that it will be acceptable; for what if it were a disappointment rather than an escape?"

Both the Prior of St. Andrew's and the Count were vexed to hear the Earl indulging his characteristic disregard of decorum, and begged him not to treat it so lightly.

"For," said the Prior, "it is a serious business, whatever may have been the incident; and the life of a young man, hitherto unblamable, will probably be forfeited."

The Queen having, notwithstanding the lateness of the hour, consented to receive the address, the gallery was soon thinned, and only Southennan and Rizzio were left in it. Something had all the evening dissatisfied Southennan with the conduct of Rizzio, and he felt shocked when the Italian said heartlessly,

"It is an ill wind that blows nobody good. By this rashness of Chatelard the road is open to you with Adelaide."

Southennan, though this had occurred to himself, and had even subdued, in some degree, his regret for the fate which the Frenchman had brought upon himself, was yet not pleased to hear it so familiarly uttered, and replied sarcastically,

"It certainly seems to give you pleasure also; more than I can account for, or easily comprehend."

Rizzio perceived that he had gone farther

than the sympathy of Southennan would follow, and he was too deeply read in the mystery of man to indulge his exultation more openly. Accordingly, to avoid farther observation he soon after retired for the night: our hero also proceeded home.

On issuing from the portal of the Palace Southennan found a vast miscellaneous multitude assembled, discussing the affair with all those customary exaggerations which belong, as matters of course, to the accidents and indiscretions of princes. But he did not linger to set any of them right; for the state of excitement in which he had been held for so many hours had exhausted his strength.

The dawn was just then beginning to brighten over " the east neuk of Fife," and to shed its silvery twilight on the pinnacles and chimney-tops of the city, but the stillness of the morning was banished. The whole town was astir; men in arms were parading in all directions; the wynds were guarded; and the fearful din of warlike preparation rung around, as if the walls were actually beleaguered. A trumpet sounded

at intervals wildly from the castle, drums were beating in the hollows of the Grassmarket and the Cowgate. The surrounding country was roused. Horsemen came galloping in, followed by numerous bands of cottars and farmers, armed with such weapons as they could reach or snatch in their haste. Nor was the alarm confined to those who girded themselves for battle. When the press of patriots, who thronged the gates and filled the streets, began to slacken, carles of more forethought were seen approaching, seated on carts and wains loaded with provisions; and long trains of pack-horses, laden with sacks of meal, driven by boys, displayed the national sagacity in turning all accidents to profitable account; these were soon after followed by coveys of country wives and lasses, with creels on their arms: circumstances which, while all around menaced tumult, indicated a general persuasion that it would come to no head. The universal scene was not unlike a multitudinous fair. Nor did the influx and commotion soon cease, for the tidings of the Queen's danger spread far and wide, insomuch that those who

came first into the city could hardly find room to repass the gates, against the crowd that was streaming in. The alarm was interesting to others besides the populace. The Reformers and the Catholics heard it with equal consternation, and from all quarters hastened to the scene. The Protestants came flocking like doves to the windows, and the Papists like crows and ravens to the new-turned fields, where they had of old been accustomed to pillage.

CHAPTER XXX.

*" The dream's here still; even when I wake, it is
Without me as within me; not imagined, felt."*
CYMBELINE.

When Knockwhinnie heard what had happened to Chatelard, he came to consult with our hero. He was disappointed by the discovery of the true object of Chatelard's affections; it made him feel a degree of resentment at what he regarded as a deception; but he still recollected with gratitude the debt he owed him for having procured his pardon; and the object of his visit was to ask Southennan to accompany him to the place where the unfortunate Frenchman was confined.

" Though," said Knockwhinnie, " I am not content with him for having so openly and ardently professed an attachment for my daugh-

ter, yet in return for the obligations he has laid me under, it is my duty to endeavour by all imaginable means, consistent with integrity, to mitigate his afflictions."

Southennan readily acquiesced in his request, and they proceeded down to the Palace, where they were informed that Chatelard had been removed to the Castle.

Adelaide was ill, and could not be seen. Her father, however, requested that she would allow him to see her, and he was admitted. He had expected to find her afflicted with grief, and her disease only agitation; but, on walking into the room, he was surprised to see her sitting alone, and that she took no notice of his entrance. He spoke to her, first chidingly, for yielding to such extreme grief, and then tenderly exhorted her to make an effort to regain her tranquillity. But she heeded not what he said, and he became alarmed at the vacuity of her eyes and the paleness of her countenance. It was manifest that her mind was overwhelmed by one dreadful idea, and that she was in no condition to be left alone.

"This is too much," said he; "it can neither be justified nor indulged, that you should abandon yourself to such sorrow."

Her answer showed the fearful idea with which she was possessed.

"He will be executed! the Queen will not interfere!"

"Of what avail, then, is grief?" replied her father. "The better part for you is to remain quiet; it is also the more comely. How hopeless your regard for him has ever been!"

Without seeming in any degree moved, and still sitting with the same stedfast and pale vacant countenance, she said,

"He will be executed! the Queen will not interfere!"

"You heed me not!" exclaimed her father, tenderly taking her by the hand. "Why do you but repeat these words? I beseech, you, Adelaide, to answer me, and not to sit with that mournful look."

"He will be executed! the Queen will not interfere!"

This repetition deeply affected Knockwhin-

nie: he chafed her hand, and, otherwise endeavouring to rouse her, called her earnestly by name as if she had been asleep; but her catalepsy was too intense to be disturbed by his endeavours. He summoned assistance, and searched for essences, or any of the other means by which sensibility is usually recalled; but neither his fears nor his cares excited her attention. She sat in the same attitude, her hand resting on her knee as he left it: her eyes continued in the same glassy stare, and void of speculation. Her attendant, who had quitted the apartment when she had admitted him, returned, and, on seeing her condition, screamed, and flew upon her in a state of distraction, fearing she was dead. All produced no effect; for, even while Annette, her maid, was weeping and lamenting over her, she said, with the same appalling and corpse-like calm,

" He will be executed! the Queen will not interfere!"

" What does she mean by repeating these words?"

" They are those," replied Annette, " of the

Lady Mary Livingstone, when she told her that Chatelard was removed to the Castle."

The mention of his name seemed to produce some impression on Adelaide; for she turned her head round, and looked as if her consciousness were reviving. Her father, on seeing this, stood eagerly watching her recovery; and Annette, with folded hands, also stood looking with terror in her face, as if she too watched some inconceivable change.

"The bell is tolling, and the crowd gathering!" said Adelaide.

A slight hectical glow shone for a moment on her alabaster cheek; and the colour, which began to return to her lips, continued to deepen to the natural coral; her eyes, however, were still motionless:

"Who is that sallow gaunt wretch, whose lean arms are bared to the shoulders?"

"What does she mean?"

"She is thinking of the executioner," replied Annette. "Hush! she speaks again!"

"They are coming! That felon-looking wretch carries his axe as proudly as a truncheon

of honour. Their heads are rising! now they have come up upon the scaffold! they move apart! Oh, Chatelard!" she exclaimed, with a violent shriek, and, starting from her chair, seemed like one that had awakened from the incantations of the night-mare.

"My child! my child!" cried her father, embracing her.

Without, however, appearing to be sensible of his presence, she said,

"Where have I been? Was I asleep, and but dreamt? Oh! such perfect visions come not in sleep." And, tears rushing into her eyes, she wept for some time, gradually recovering. Still, without noticing her father, she said,

"Annette! why put I on this mantle? Where did I intend to go?" And, with a momentary glare of wildness, she suddenly turned to her father, and exclaimed,—

"Were you not speaking, sir? Did you not chide me?"

"Alas, my pretty Adelaide, I had not then observed thy condition! But compose thyself."

"I begin to have some recollection," said she,

in a strange hollow voice, "that Mary Livingstone came to me, and said that Chatelard was taken to the Castle. Did she not say, 'He will be executed, and the Queen will not interfere?' She did say that. But where is she?—and how are you here, my father?—and Annette, what would you, that you stand gazing, as if there were something fearful upon me?"

At this crisis, the Lady Mary Livingstone entered from another apartment, followed by the physician of the palace; and by his orders Knockwhinnie went into the adjoining room, accompanied by the Lady Mary, from whom he learned, that just before he had been admitted, and while she was telling her of the Queen's inexorable determination, Adelaide suddenly fell into that frightful syncope.

The physician presently joined them, and assured Knockwhinnie that quiet and repose would soon restore his daughter.

"It is but a womanly infirmity that has overtaken her; and with the help of a little sleep, she will soon be well again. There is no medicament more salutary in such a case."—

Southennan, in the meantime, had met the Count in the gallery, coming from the Queen, with an appearance of satisfaction so obvious, that he could not but inquire the cause of his apparent enjoyment.

" Her Majesty," replied Duffroy, " surprises me. With all the vacillations of her sex, she is this morning more firm in her purpose than I have ever seen her before; for, spite of the struggle between her mercy, or it may be regard for Chatelard, and her dignity, she is still resolute to let the law take its course."

" Then," said Southennan, " you will suspend your return to France?"

" Yes, but not altogether of my own resolution; for she has commanded me to remain, upon a promise that I made to her uncles, the Princes of Lorrain, to continue with her, until she should select a suitable husband and protector. Although my task here ill accords with my inclinations, yet I cannot forget the solemnity of my promise, so long as I can do any service not inconsistent with my honour. I do not think now that she entertains any affection for the rash

young man, or was privy to his criminal folly. Had she been so, I would have taken my departure by the same vessel this day in which he was to have sailed; but now I will continue yet awhile, and particularly as she has for the first time intimated her intention of chusing a husband. It is needful; and there is wisdom in the suggestion occurring to her at this time. Moreover, she has raised Rizzio, not only to fill the place of Chatelard in the Chancery, but to manage the correspondence with the princes of Europe regarding her intention to marry; a trust of great delicacy, which could not be in abler hands. I would it were in honester!"

"If you doubt his honesty, my Lord Count, why have you approved of the appointment?"

"I do not mean honesty, as it is spoken of by traders and burghers; but of that sort which does not too eagerly look for advantages to its possessor. In sooth, I think Rizzio is one who will, in chusing a husband for the Queen, chuse also a patron for himself; and by that she may suffer."

"If you think so, why, permit me to say again, have you not told the Queen this?"

"I have," said the Count; "but she is wilful; and I am too happy to find her so well inclined to vindicate herself and dignity, in this affair of Chatelard, that I postponed my stronger remonstrance until some more convenient season."

CHAPTER XXXI.

"He jests at scars who never felt a wound!"
ROMEO AND JULIET.

SOUTHENNAN and Knockwhinnie having obtained an order to admit them to Chatelard, left the Palace together, and proceeded up towards the Castle. As they were walking along, Southennan, without acquainting his companion that he knew where Auchenbrae was secreted, inquired if he still cherished his anger against him.

"Knockwhinnie," said he, "now you have happily obtained your own pardon, it were as well to think no more of the injuries which you have suffered, but to allow the wounds of your mind to heal."

"It is easy for you to say so; it is easy for those who never knew danger or difficulty to

give brave advice; it is easy for those who have not felt misfortune themselves, to descant on the faults of the unhappy. I grant that I was rash in my revenge on Count Dufroy; but neither in principle nor motive was it unjust; and therefore, though he was innocent, and I repent my rashness towards him, yet the guilt which provoked my dagger, deserved the punishment I intended. My conscience will not be satisfied, if justice be not done!"

Southennan was too much under the influence of the spirit of the age to be sensible to the peril of that doctrine. His own nature, frank and generous, was not likely to be instigated by fierce feelings, even under a sense of injury; but he considered not with sufficient antipathy the license which was too generally assumed by injured individuals, personally to redress their own wrongs. He was, in consequence, not apt to controvert the notions of Knockwhinnie either eagerly or with much force; he only observed in reply—

" The revival of old grudges seldom does any good; the guilt of Auchenbrae was much similar

to your own attempt on the Count, in the wrong he did your house; it was not successful, and as you have obtained your pardon because your own intention had not been accomplished, for the same reason you should consider whether you ought not, in your turn, to pardon him."

"The cases are not parallel; his injury to me and mine was dictated by his own profligacy: I had never given him any cause to justify the wrong he did. In him it was pure wickedness; my attempt on the Count was as guiltless as an accident; I believed him to have committed the injuries that have blasted my life, but as he was innocent of them I could have no reason in doing what I did. When the truth was known the Count was changed in my thoughts from a debtor to a creditor. I owed him for the harm I had done him, as it were, in mistake."

"Then you are still determined to avenge the wrong you have suffered by Auchenbrae?"

"I do not say," replied Knockwhinnie, "that I will in his case take the law into my own

hands, because he has long been addicted to habits and practices that have cut him off from the fellowship of gentlemen. Moreover, I have consulted my kinsman, Lord Killiecrankie, of the Court of Sesssion, and he is of opinion that I would unworthily demean myself were I to take the punishment upon myself; and, moreover, he also says, if I prosecuted him in the Court, I would have great difficulty in maintaining my case for lack of sufficient evidence; and that, as his Lordship said, is the only reason which could justify me in taking upon myself to make good what the law cannot reach."

Southennan was perplexed at hearing this, and observed—

" What would he say if you killed Auchenbrae, and were brought before his Lordship for murder?"

" Really," replied Knockwhinnie, " that is a point of law which neither of us thought of!"

As they were thus talking, and occasionally stopping to recover their breath, exhausted in climbing the steep ascent between the Netherbow and the Castle, Johnnie Gaff, who had ob-

served them together, followed at a respectful distance along the side of the street, plainly indicating by his frequent glances at Knockwhinnie, a desire to be noticed by his old master.

Johnnie was an altered man; he had lost, by his dismissal from the halberdiers, not only his uniform but much of his self-consequence. This was the more severely felt, as the streets were thronged with crowds of armed rustics whom the alarm had brought in from the country, among whom Johnnie felt his habitual desire to vindicate authority again revived. He was also a good deal annoyed by idle children, who, recognising him in his more homely apparel, sometimes, to shew the natural satisfaction of humanity at the sight of fallen greatness, pushed him about, and treated him with all the derision so generally rendered to misfortune.

At last Johnnie caught the eye of Knockwhinnie; before whom, cap-in-hand, he immediately presented himself. At first, in his altered garb he was not recognized, but he soon took care to be so.

"It's true, Knockwhinnie," said he, "that the *ony probandy* lies on me to convince you that I am John Gaff, umquhile clerk to Mathew Symington, heretofore your Baron Bailie."

"Ah!" exclaimed Knockwhinnie, "I am glad to see you."

"Thank you, Knockwhinnie; and if I can be o' any service now that I'm out o' bread, I'm willing, *sirty mory*."

Knockwhinnie was at the time in want of a servant, and the idea occurred to him that Johnnie might be useful. He laughed, however, at the offer, and said—

"I see, Johnnie that what is bred in the bone is not easily got out of the flesh: you are as modest as ever. After seizing me by the neck with so little reverence, how can you think that I should endure you in my service again?"

"Na, Knockwhinnie, that ought to be a reason for taking me: it's an *argumenty ad hominy;* for I but did my duty to the Lord Provost and the Queen, and it's as gude as a written testificate, that I'm likely to be as trusty in

the servitude o' ither folk. I was in the lawful exercise of my calling and jurisdiction; and for that, Knockwhinnie, ye should treat with me on the *state of anty Bell.*"

" Well, Johnnie, come to the Unicorn after dinner, and we shall have a negociation."

" But," replied Johnnie, " I see ye 're on some intent o' business. Now, as I 'm weel acquaint wi' the *locus loci* of ilk wynd and closs; indeed, I may say, I ken *totas et integras* every hole and corner o' the burgh o' Embro; couldna ye find a bit turn for me to do afore the afternoon?"

Knockwhinnie laughed, and replied,

" All I have to do, I must do myself!"

Southennan here suggested that as Johnnie had held so recently an official appointment, he might be serviceable in conducting them through the Castle to the tower in which Chatelard was confined; and the suggestion being adopted, Johnnie was directed to follow them.

It would have been instructive to the student of mankind to have seen the immediate effect which the acceptance of Johnnie's services pro-

duced on him. The shy and diffident air with which, though affecting freedom, he had addressed himself to his quondam master, instantly disappeared; and he only seemed in want of his halberd, to be as dignified as ever. Indeed it was a great lack to be then without, for as he erected himself into official importance, his hands and arms were awkwardly cumbersome : a switch would at that time have improved his stiff graces. However, he drew confidence from his vocation ; and did not, as they walked to the Castle-hill, fail to give a glowing impression of his palm on the cheek of more than one of the urchins who held out their fingers as he passed, and molested him with their murgeons.

At the Castle-gate, Johnnie showed that he knew how to set about his business, by telling his master and Southennan to wait at the drawbridge, while he went in to ascertain from the sentries if admission would be allowed; greatly, however, to Johnnie's discomfiture, he was gruffly told to go about his business, for nobody could be admitted without an order.

"I'm very sorry," said he, as he came out,

"that ye hae climbed the hill to sae little purpose. Had I no been *functy offeeshy*, I could hae ta'en you in without a *mandamus*."

" We have one," replied Knockwhinnie; " and here it is!"

" Then, *instanty perit* a' difficulty." On saying which, Johnnie took the paper, and proudly leading the van, showed it with an air to the soldier; and, without condescending to exchange a word, proceeded up the ascent to the next gate, which he passed with equal silence and ceremony. On reaching the higher court, where a number of the garrison were playing at penny stanes, Johnnie procured a soldier to conduct them to Chatelard's prison, where they had not long to remain, until an old man came with the keys.

The jailor had been, in his better days, of great athletic power: age had diminished both the quantity and the articulation of his flesh and muscles; but his joints were gnarled and unusually large, and his hands huge, and roped with veins and sinews, even to a degree that still implied the possession of Herculean strength. He stooped

beneath the burden of age; his hoary head was uncovered; and though his office was stern, there was yet no sullenness in his countenance: on the contrary, his eyes were lively, and his look cheerful, even facetious. He came leaning on a staff, and carried in his hand three or four large rusty keys; one of which he applied to the lock, and admitted the visitors.

CHAPTER XXXII.

> —————— " I see men's judgments are
> A parcel of their fortunes; and things outward
> Do draw the inward quality after them
> To suffer all alike."
> ANTHONY AND CLEOPATRA.

THE full danger of his situation did not occur to the apprehension of Chatelard, until he was conducted from the Palace to the Castle; for although, when he was first discovered, his consternation was great and visible, it did not last long. His vanity suggested that the Queen would soon relent; and with this imaginary assurance he comforted himself till he was brought before the Council: even there, hope did not desert him; and he thought that the rough humour of the Earl of Morton was not an omen to be dreaded. After his removal from the Council the flattery continued; and he was no otherwise treated

while he remained under custody in Holyrood House than as usual, with the exception of the guards in the room with him. But in the morning, when he was informed that a litter was in waiting, in which he was to be conveyed to the Castle, the cold touch of fear made him shudder. Still it was observed, that although he was slightly agitated as he mounted the litter, he yet showed no pusillanimity or terror of punishment. But when, as he was carried up the street, he beheld the vast multitude rolling on all sides like the waves of the sea, and saw the universal alarm in every countenance, he became sad and spiritless. He was then convinced of the extent of public disaster which his folly involved, and that he was passing from beyond the reach of his imaginary influence with the Queen.

On arriving at the Castle Hill, he beheld a number of the garrison drawn out, and a great crowd assembled: the soldiers, as the litter moved towards the gate, formed a circle round it to keep off the people; it halted at the drawbridge, on which he alighted, and he was con-

ducted by the troops across. The instant he was within the portal, the bridge was raised and the portcullis dropped, with a clang which sounded in his ears more awful than thunder. He felt as if the gates of life were shut upon him, and his agitation became so great, that he was obliged to lean on the arm of the officer who conducted him to the traitor's room. From a sentiment of compassion, the officer offered to remain with him; but he declined the civility, and begged, with a husky throat, that he would send him a draught of water. In this he was indulged; and the officer, after an ineffectual attempt to cheer him, left him with his despair.

For some time he remained immoveable: the noise of the agitated city rung in his ears like the voice of the ocean in a storm: sometimes it seemed to subside, and to sink as if tranquillity were spreading; but ever and anon it rose with a terrible burst, as if the confusion of cataracts and earthquakes was raging around. But the tension of the indescribable feeling from which he so suffered was too excessive to afflict him long, and he became sensible that his condition

was not to be lightened by yielding to unmanly alarms; accordingly, he made an effort to rouse himself, and it was not unsuccessful.

The apartment in which he was confined was appropriated exclusively to state prisoners; it was in one of the highest towers, and was lighted by a grated window, which looked towards the west. No part of the town could be seen from it, but in other respects the view was extensive and cheerful.

The apartment itself was not uncomfortable: three tall narrow-backed chairs stood at one side; a large settle, or wooden settee, occupied a space opposite; and the bed was in a niche; a table, ponderous and massy, occupied the middle of the room; and a huge carved oaken chest, with brazen hinges, and a vast brazen lock, stood under the window.

When he had looked abroad upon the western landscape, his mind received, from its brightness and tranquillity, a sympathetic sentiment of clearness and calm. He had been unable, during the whole night previous, although in comparative self-possession, to collect his

thoughts. The tablets of his memory were disordered and broken: he had a vivid remembrance of every thing which had taken place, but could not arrange them, either in the order of time, or connect them easily with minor circumstances.

The chaos of his thoughts, in the transit from the Palace to the Castle, admitted of no order: they were feelings something more like corporeal pains and pangs than mental recollections. But as he became more composed the storm abated, and the wreck of his thoughts drifted with less and less violence.

On retiring from the window he threw his eyes round the room, and saw on several parts of the pannels names and inscriptions, the memorials of former prisoners. Some of the names he had heard of, and that those who possessed them had all perished on the scaffold. The inscriptions were equally dismal: they expressed regrets and sorrow, and complained of unfaithful friends.

The recollection of the advice he had received from Rizzio, and which in the delusion of hope

and vanity he had adopted, flashed upon him, and the peril into which he had in consequence fallen seemed strikingly in accordance with the result predicted to those who did not attend to the admonitions in the inscriptions. The suspicion of the Italian's integrity being once awakened, his memory ran over innumerable records, unconsciously placed among her archives, which ought, had they been rightly heeded, to have preserved him from following his subtle and insidious advice.

"He will thrive," exclaimed Chatelard, "by my ruin. Had he not set me on, I never should have dared to risk myself until I had received some plainer proof that the Queen was willing to accept my love: but I was infatuated, else I should have seen how craftily he had paved the way by which I have been brought here."

In thus blaming his own weakness in yielding to advice that bore in its very object a certainty of great danger, he could not refrain from uttering with vehemence threats of vengeance against his perfidious friend. But in his passion he

forgot his own condition; and when the recollection of it returned upon him, he was overwhelmed with a horror darker and wilder than all he had yet suffered.

The humiliation of being deprived of the means of revenge was in itself dreadful. He felt as a man enraged, whose hands have been smitten with paralysis; his ineffectual indignation was as the storming of a child against the stone that has hurt it; and he was seized with a fit of convulsive laughter at the mere imagination of throwing the javelin, his arm more incapable by his fetters than had it been withered by old age.

It was during this paroxysm that he heard the key turned in the lock to admit Southennan and Knockwhinnie. The sound roused him from the aimless rage of his despair, and he prepared himself to receive whoever the visitors might be, with at least some outward show of equanimity. But no effort of resolution could prevent them from discovering that he had undergone, since the preceding evening, a dismal and appalling change. His complexion was

faded into an ashy wanness; his eyes were sunken, and his cheeks hollow; his hair was matted and oily, with the sweat of felonious agitation; he looked many years older; and there was a premature cast of the cadavre in his countenance, that rendered his appearance almost terrible. He, however, received them with a hysterical cheerfulness. Knockwhinnie, instead of answering his expressions of joy, looked at Southennan, who, not less distressed, sat down unbidden, and said to himself,

"I was not prepared for this. Pardon me, Chatelard; but I had not imagined it possible, that in so few hours you could have been so altered!"

Chatelard endeavoured to laugh, but it was more like a hideous rattle than the expression of any cheerful feeling, as he said—

"True; I have not had time to make my toilet: and I assure you, that the toil of a traitor's thoughts is as hard as a soldier's in battle."

Knockwhinnie by this time had also taken a seat, but he was still so grieved and amazed

that he could find no terms to express what he felt. Each, however, soon became sensible that the indulgence of dejection was not becoming to the occasion, and they severally rallied themselves into a more masculine mood.

CHAPTER XXXIII.

*" For neither man nor angel can discern
Hypocrisy ; the only evil that walks
Invisible, except to God alone."*
MILTON.

THE state of Rizzio's mind was in the meantime not enviable. In advising Chatelard to that boldness which had precipitated his fate, the Italian had never imagined his rashness would carry him to such an extremity as to violate the sanctuary of the Queen's chamber. He had only anticipated some indiscretion which would have the effect of removing him from her Majesty's service; but when he witnessed the public consternation which the discovery had produced, he perceived that the consequences could not be calculated, and it filled him with anxiety and dread. He was as the simpleton in the forest, who for some petty

personal advantage, throws a fire-brand into the brake, and beholds in consequence a hurricane of flames rising, and raging to a general conflagration of the woods.

But he had so conducted himself, from the time that Chatelard was ordered to quit the kingdom, as to avert all suspicion of having abetted him in his purpose; still his astonishment at the disastrous result was not greater than his grief; for the indignation of the Queen, the severe determination of the Council, and, above all, the tumultuous and universal rage of the people, rendered an ignominious doom inevitable. There was, indeed, no affectation of sorrow in the pity of Rizzio; on the contrary, it was sharpened with contrition; for he could not hide from himself, that his advice had doubtless ministered to the ruin by which Chatelard was overtaken. Ambition was in Rizzio his strongest energy, but he possessed many of the generous qualities which are usually found in connection with that gorgeous passion. These induced him to attempt the almost hopeless task of appeasing the anger of the household,

and particularly to address himself to such members of the Privy Council with whom he had acquired the privilege of expressing any opinion.

His first endeavour was with the Prior of St. Andrews; for, instructed by his innate discernment of character, he rightly considered, that although the object of his suit was merciful, it was yet one on which the Queen could not be addressed, even by her ladies; whilst it was precisely, in all its bearings, a case wherein the interference of the Prior could be most becomingly exercised.

Accordingly, without seeking an opportunity, he availed himself of the first afforded to speak on the subject: it took place much about the time that Knockwhinnie and Southennan were with the prisoner. The Prior had come to pay his morning respects to her Majesty, and until she was ready to receive him, he happened, without any particular motive, to go into the room where Rizzio was already preparing despatches to the different ministers abroad, to intimate to the respective courts at which they

were stationed, her Majesty's intention of again entertaining proposals of marriage.

Rizzio mentioned to him the purport of the letters, and then, with his wonted dexterity, alluded to the folly of Chatelard, applying to it, with equal skill and address, the softest epithets he could select, in order insensibly to soften the indignation it had inspired into some more lenient feeling.

" But for the consequences to the unfortunate man himself," said the Italian, " none can regret the indecorum of his rashness, since it has been the means of bringing her Majesty to this resolution, so greatly desired by all her servants and subjects. I only regret that the rigour of the Scottish laws may require a sacrifice disproportioned to the extent of Chatelard's guilt. It will be an ill omen, if the nuptials must be celebrated with blood."

" Heaven forfend it," replied the Prior, " but the fate of the traitor will be consummated long enough before any match can be agreed on."

" I hope," said Rizzio, " though his rashness cannot be pardoned, it is not of so deep a dye

as treason, and that death will not follow of necessity. No ill has resulted from it, but to poor Chatelard himself. It is but a thin partition which divides unfulfilled intention from innocence."

"You are too subtle, Rizzio: it is not wholesome to morality to draw such fine conclusions: for it is the will that makes the guilt of a purpose; and a frustrated intent loses none of its sinfulness by having been frustrated."

"I have neither skill nor casuistry enough," replied Rizzio, "to debate with my Lord Prior; but perhaps, before Chatelard was discovered, he may have rued his indiscretion; and does not such repentance redeem innocence?"

"You speak of him," said the Prior, "with more temperance than may be done unblamed."

"In truth, my Lord, I cannot else but lament the jeopardy into which he has fallen. He is possessed of many talents, and, save in this most perilous misfortune, was singularly unblemished. His unremitted study, until the constraint of destiny brought him, ill fated, to Scotland, was to improve those gifts with which Heaven had

been pleased to endow him so richly; and, but for this woful infatuation, he was one that would have proved himself an ornament to mankind. I hope it is no fault that I lament the temerity of his fond passion. Alas! it does seem hard that too ardent love should be sin against loyalty. What more than the doom it is said he must suffer, could have been his fate, had he meditated the use of the traitor's dagger on the Queen's life?—yea, had he, with the rancour of real treason, actually plunged it into her bosom? Ah, my Lord! look on his frailty as it is seen by Nature; and, for a time, forget the artificial guilt which the law, in its austerity, hath invented to gratify the prejudices of society. He has been betrayed by love; and is not love the life of society—the very element and essence of the prime duty of man? It may be that the tears of sorrowful friendship make me blind; but neither guilt nor sin can I discern in Chatelard's misdemeanour, but only more of virtue than stands within the approbation of the narrow and unpitying law."

"It were wise of you, Rizzio, not to speak

after this manner to the Earl of Morton, and wiser if you did not speak at all; for it stands not within the possibility of duty to herself, or to her dignity, that the Queen's mercy can reach Chatelard."

At this point of their conversation, the Prior was summoned to attend her Majesty, and the Italian left to ruminate on the failure of his mediation. He was not, however, disheartened: disappointment proved often to him a goad to endeavour; and in this case it was particularly so. He was not only incited to perseverance by regret for the fearful situation in which the victim of his advice stood, but also by something like pique at his ingenuity proving so abortive; for, like many others of that period, he was deceived, by the general gentleness of the Prior's manners, into a belief that he possessed less stability of principle than he afterwards manifested; and in consequence he was led to presume that he might influence him by a course of argument relative to principles seldom applicable to the controversies of courtiers, with whom the right, and the abstract merit of necessity, always give

way to the expedient. But his management was different with the Earl of Morton, who shortly after entered his room, and whose coarser character required a more worldly treatment. He accordingly set roundly to work with him; for the familiar and jocose habits of the Earl encouraged him to take that liberty. But Morton, like many who freely indulge themselves in jocularity with others, did not much like to be the object of it from them in return; and thus it happened, that although none of the Privy Council had formed a more correct estimate of the talents and character of Rizzio, few of them had so great a distaste to him, arising entirely from the presumption with which he appeared, in conversation, to rank himself as an equal.

CHAPTER XXXIV.

"There 's a divinity that shapes our ends,
Rough-hew them how we will."
SHAKSPEARE.

"WEEL, Dauvit!" said the Earl of Morton to Rizzio, after some general prelude touching the matter, "What think ye will be the upshot of this straemash? The Frenchman, puir chield! I doot, is past redemption; for I hae been discoursing with that bardy scoot, the Leddy Mall Livingstone; and if she would hae gi'en me the minimumest inkling that the Queen's Majesty had been either by hook or crook privy to the fallow's derning himself aneath the bed, I would hae stood up for him in the face and teeth o' the boldest at the Council-Board; for it's awfu' to think o' putting a spirity lad's head in a tow for

falling in love wi' a bonny young wanton widow."

"That's said like yourself, my Lord," replied Rizzio. "Not one of all the Council have a right conception of the case."

"Foggies!" exclaimed Morton; "Where could they get it? There's no' ane amang them, Dauvit, that has as meikle daft blood in his tail as a sybow, tho' they dinna want smeddum to make the e'en water, whether it be a case o' guilt or innocence. But I'm mair provoked at Prior Jamie than any other; for he's a douce young man, and it's weel kent that chields of that sort are Solomons amang the lasses. In sooth, Dauvit, it does not consort with my conceit of state wisdom to look overly curious aneath the Queen's bed or blankets. Puir forlorn young widow! it's no' decent to make such a hobbleshow; for after a', she may have been really diverting hersel'."

"Your Lordship," replied Rizzio, "takes a plain and honest view of the matter. You see it with the spectacles of experience. Justice surely would be satisfied, were Chatelard sent out of the kingdom."

" That's sensible, Dauvit. Really thou's a clever deevil—I'll ay say that o' thee. But the Queen hersel' is the worst of a'. It's an unco' thing to hear o' folk so fond o' blood: nae doubt it comes of Papistry; for when I was in that delusion, Gude forgie me! I had a kind of heart-felt satisfaction in seeing a head chappit aff, especially when the axe was blunt, and the job was hagglet: it gart me grind my teeth with a feeling like fainness."

" Your Lordship could not better show the mercifulness of your reformed nature than by your compassion for Chatelard. I grieve to think his case is so hopeless. Perhaps, however, when the trial is over, your interposition then may be more effectual."

" But what fashes me most about it," replied the Earl, " is the marvelling it may breed abroad. We'll just be laughed at for being o' sic a maidenly morality."

" It may deter the princes"—

" Pa, pa! Dauvit, gie thysel' nae concern about them. What cares a kiesor o' Almaigne, or an Italian hircos, about sic a

stale commodity as chastity? It would ne'er hae been a mot in the Queen's marriage wi' the best o' them, had Chatelard been catched cuddling in her bosom. But, Dauvit, I redde ye tak' tent what ye do anent this matter o' the marriage; for we'll no allow our hiefer to mell wi' far aff cattle. Scotland's no to become a pendicle to another kingdom. So ye'll ne'er let wot to the Imperator, nor to Philip o' Spain, that the Queen's a wanter; but fin' out some canny princie, in straightened circumstances, that will be thankful for his promotion, and biddable to the barons and 'states o' the realm."

With this advice the Earl retired to attend her Majesty in the Council Chamber, where Rizzio soon after presented himself with the drafts of the letters he had been directed to prepare, and received not only the Queen's commendations for the elegance of the diction, but also the applause of more than one of the counsellors for being a fairer writer than his predecessor.

"It behoves us now," said the Earl of Morton,

"to consider to what courts the letters should be sent; for it's my notion, please your Majesty, that the dignity of this your ancient realm will be best maintained by waling your gudeman frae out the lesser princes of Christendom: for it was a great fear among us a', that had your Majesty been graciously pleased to bear a bairn to the French king, Scotland might have become a commodity to France, and been dragged through nae better than dirt and defamation until her royalty was utterly destroyed."

In this patriotic sentiment the whole Council concurred; and the Queen assured them that she would leave the choice entirely to them, for she had no doubt they would see well to the weal of the state, and she added, with a smile to the Earl of Morton, that she trusted her personal happiness would not be forgotten.

"Your Majesty," said the Earl, "need gie yoursel' nae concern about that; for as it's no' a king we hae to look for, but only a solacium for your widowhood, our first duty will be to please you; and, therefore, I trust my noble

friends here will no be overly scrupulous anent the talents of the prince, but look to the parts of the man. Indeed, clever princes, which, thanks be praise! are no' common, hae seldom been a convenience in Scotland; and as we are content with your Majesty's great power and capacity for ruling a camstairie people, we'll make choice o' a weel faur't man o' a moderate capacity."

When this part of the deliberation was over, her Majesty retired, and the Council proceeded to issue the necessary orders for the trial of Chatelard, and they were carried into effect next day; for, as Lord Morton said,

" Since ye will put him to death, there's Christianity in putting him out o' pain wi' a' reasonable expedition."

After this the Council broke up, and Morton, who was never perfectly satisfied of the Queen's entire innocence, resolved to visit the prisoner; accordingly, on leaving the Palace, he proceeded straight to the Castle, and was admitted to Chatelard while Southennan and Knockwhinnie were still with him.

"Gentlemen," said he to them as he entered, "I maun beg you to let me be alone wi' this puir lad. His time's fast coming, for the morn is set for his trial, and maybe he would be nane the waur o' making a bit shrift to me before appearing at the bar. I hope I'm breaking in on nae more interesting business."

In this short address there was somewhat more of gravity than in the Earl's usual manner; for he really thought that the affair was magnified beyond the guilt of it.

Knockwhinnie and Southennan accordingly left the prisoner, promising to see him again, and encouraging him to keep up his spirits; for since a trial had been granted, there was still a chance of some mitigation of the penalty he had incurred.

As soon as they were out of the room, the Earl said—

"It's but a fule's counsel, my man, that they hae gi'en you: ye hae nae better ground o' hope than that ye hae to deal wi' a weathercock woman; though, to do her justice in this matter, she's doure enough. However, sit

down beside me, and tell me truly a' the outs and ins o' your exploit; for save that crooked spirit, Dauvit, I dinna' think ye hae a true frien' beside mysel'."

" I fear," replied Chatelard, " that I can count but little on the friendship of Rizzio."

" Ay, man; what reason hae ye for saying sae? for really, though I dinna' think him a' thegither a creature o' perfect sincerity, I'm sure he has a warm side to you, and nae man could make lighter o' your offence, or plead stronger for indulgence to you than he did to me this morning. What can be the thought that makes you suspect his truth?"

" Because, had he not incited me to obtrude upon the Queen, it would never have entered my imagination."

" Oh, the scoun'rel! Did he do that? My word, it was a supple trick; for by it he has whisked you to the wuddy, and himsel' into your office. Howsoever, just be plain with me, Monsieur, and I'll no slacken in my endeavour for your behoof. Tell me truly, had ye any en-

couragement frae the Queen's Majesty to do what ye did?"

"Not by word, certainly."

"Na," replied the Earl, "she's o'er cunning a hen to speak; that would be Lathron-like: but she has, nae doubt, smiled upon you, and touched your tae wi' her foot, and wi' other sweet and secret blandishments gi'en you an understanding that wasna' kittle to read."

Chatelard made no reply to this, but shook his head.

"Weel," said the Earl, "this is a knotty case: ye're really a venturesome gamester to run sic a risk without a blink o' favour."

"It was the dream and delusion of passion: I was spell-bound, and driven to it by an irresistible impulse."

"Didna' ye say, just now, that ye were eggit on by Dauvit, and now ye lay the wyte on your stars."

A good deal more conversation ensued, but it all ended in proving that Chatelard had weakly yielded too much, and gone too far on

Rizzio's advice, while it confirmed—if confirmation had been necessary—the opinion which Morton entertained of the Italian's subtlety and address, without greatly diminishing his suspicions of the Queen.

END OF VOL II.

J. B. NICHOLS, AND SON,
25, PARLIAMENT STREET.

THIS BOOK IS DUE ON THE LAST DATE STAMPED BELOW

AN INITIAL FINE OF 25 CENTS
WILL BE ASSESSED FOR FAILURE TO RETURN THIS BOOK ON THE DATE DUE. THE PENALTY WILL INCREASE TO 50 CENTS ON THE FOURTH DAY AND TO $1.00 ON THE SEVENTH DAY OVERDUE.

SEP 2 1944	
13 Feb '52 GW	
12 Feb 52 LU	
NOV 5 1978 REC. CIR. OCT 18 78	
	LD 21-100m-12,'43(8796s)

Galt, John
Southennan.

955
G179
so
v.2

SEP 2 1944 Merryfield P 1/2 19

645147

UNIVERSITY OF CALIFORNIA LIBRARY

THIS BOOK IS DUE ON THE LAST D
STAMPED BELOW

AN INITIAL FINE OF 25 CEN
WILL BE ASSESSED FOR FAILURE TO RE
THIS BOOK ON THE DATE DUE. THE PEN
WILL INCREASE TO 50 CENTS ON THE FO
DAY AND TO $1.00 ON THE SEVENTH
OVERDUE.

SEP 2 1944	
13 Feb '52 GW	
12 Feb 52 LU	
NOV 5 1978 REC. CIR. OCT 18 78	

LD 21-100m-12,'43

Galt, John
  Southennan.

955
G179
so
v.2

SEP 2 1944 Merryfield SEP 12 1944

645147

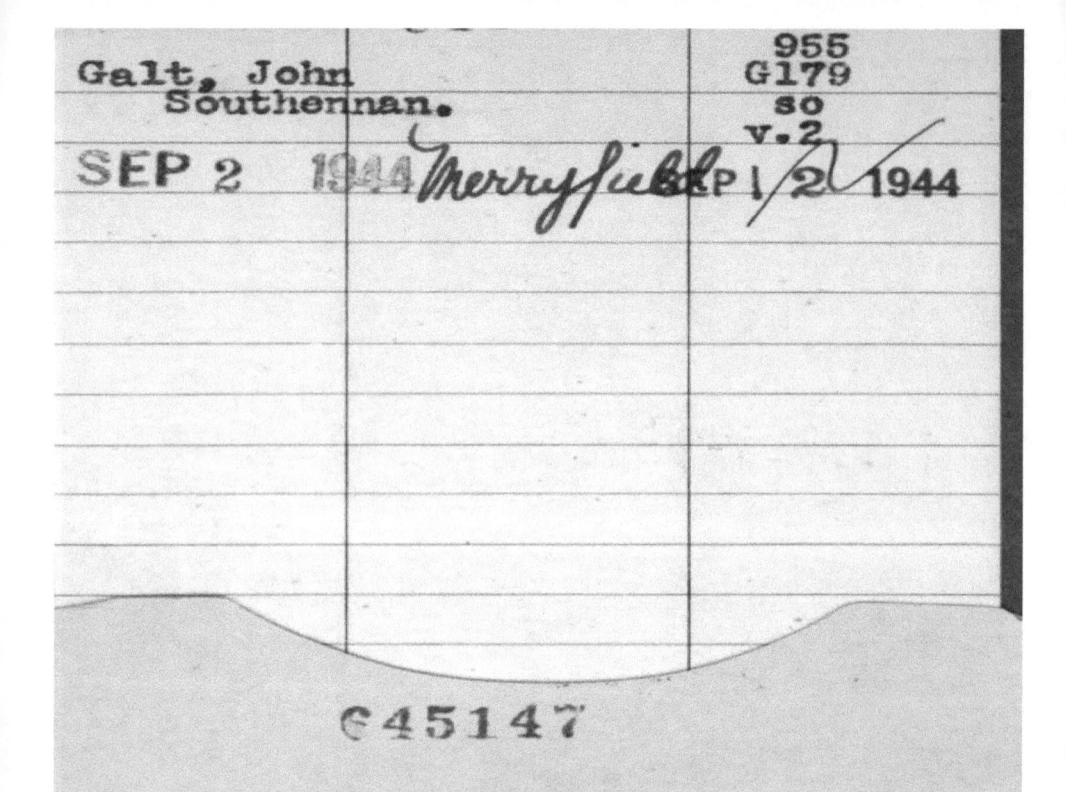

UNIVERSITY OF CALIFORNIA LIBRARY

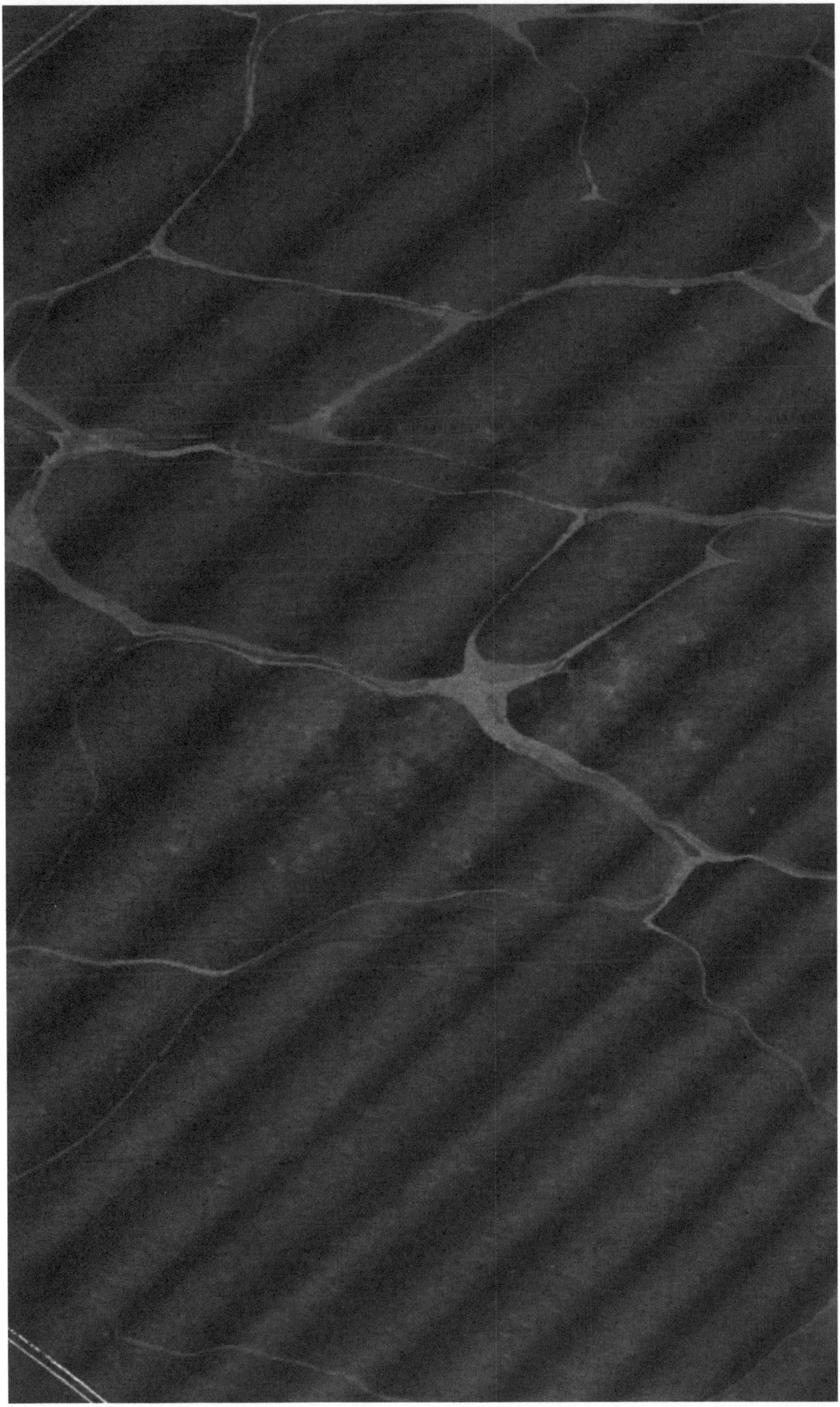

Check Out More Titles From HardPress Classics Series In this collection we are offering thousands of classic and hard to find books. This series spans a vast array of subjects – so you are bound to find something of interest to enjoy reading and learning about.

Subjects:
Architecture
Art
Biography & Autobiography
Body, Mind &Spirit
Children & Young Adult
Dramas
Education
Fiction
History
Language Arts & Disciplines
Law
Literary Collections
Music
Poetry
Psychology
Science
…and many more.

Visit us at www.hardpress.net

Im The Story
personalised classic books

"Beautiful gift.. lovely finish. My Niece loves it, so precious!"

Helen R Brumfieldon

★★★★★

JANE IN WONDERLAND

LEWIS CARROLL

UNIQUE GIFT

FOR KIDS, PARTNERS AND FRIENDS

Timeless books such as:

Kids

Alice in Wonderland • The Jungle Book • The Wonderful Wizard of Oz
Peter and Wendy • Robin Hood • The Prince and The Pauper
The Railway Children • Treasure Island • A Christmas Carol

Adults

Romeo and Juliet • Dracula

- **Highly** Customizable
- **Change** Books Title
- **Replace** Characters Names with yours
- **Upload** Photo (for inside page)
- **Add** Inscriptions

Visit **Im TheStory.com**
and order yours today!